Early Praise for
Four Weeks to Fear LESS

"*Four Weeks to Fear LESS* is a healing journey for anyone suffering from anxiety. In this practical book, the author combines self-reflection with God's soothing grace. Laura openly shares her vulnerabilities and experiences without making the reader feel judged or criticized. Her openness helps create a sense of shared experiences and allows readers to look at themselves with compassion. A wonderful read for any age group!"

Dr. Karen Swanson
Pediatrician

"*Four Weeks to Fear LESS* will transform the way you view anxiety. Laura focuses on targeting the source of fear and how to gently dismantle the walls of false protection that we have built. Packed with encouraging verses, practical tips, and thought-provoking response prompts, this journal is an essential starting place to begin embracing the freedom that comes with trusting in God's love and plans for us through our identity in Christ!"

Trinity Durham
Senior at Oconomowoc High School

"This is truly a divinely inspired book. I sense the Holy Spirit speaking through the pages, applying the truths of Scripture to the difficult circumstances that confront so many women today. We are gently guided to conform our thinking and behavior to the way of Jesus, resulting in the joy, hope, and contentment that comes only from faith and trust in him."

Terri Koschnick
Counselor and LMFT

"Laura invites us into a safe space where we can face, dismantle, and replace our fears with hope. As someone who works with young people, I found her perspective to be thoughtful, fresh, and actually helpful. Going through this journal once was not enough. There are rich treasures to unpack in this timeless collection of readings and responses that draws upon deep wisdom and grace for readers of any age."

Ellisa Lettner
Marquette University Cru Movement Leader

"Laura's witty, honest, and biblical approach invites readers to identify specific fears and make daily progress. In *Four Weeks to Fear LESS*, Laura reveals the simple but profound truth that God is ultimately the key to breaking down our walls and lessening our fear."

Sarah Balding
Business/Pre-Med Sophomore at Baylor University

"*Four Weeks to Fear LESS* is a very inspirational read that encourages those struggling with anxiety. This book honestly addresses many specific and concrete real-world issues that young adults all across the world are dealing with but are often too afraid to discuss. Sandretti writes from a sincere and honest perspective, offering her own personal experience with anxiety in order to relate to her readers. She also offers various thoughtful activities and techniques to conquer anxiety one day at a time. Most importantly, she encourages the cultivation of a relationship with Jesus Christ. This book is very powerful and teaches its readers that freedom from anxiety IS possible in the name of Jesus Christ, our Lord and Savior! As someone who struggles with anxiety myself, I found this book to be life-changing!"

Madison Zumbal
Graduate Student at Liberty University

"*Four Weeks to Fear LESS* weaves together genuine personal experiences, powerful biblical truths, and practical applications that push readers to live a life free of fear and full of confidence in the goodness of our God."

Alaina May
Business Administration & Management Junior at Boston University

*"Because of the Lord's great love
we are not consumed,
for his compassions never fail.
They are new every morning;
great is your faithfulness.
I say to myself,
'The Lord is my portion;
therefore I will wait for him.'"*

Lamentations 3:22-24

Four Weeks to Fear LESS

A 28-Day Guided Response Journal

DISCOVERING AND DISMANTLING
BARRIERS TO PEACE

Laura E. Sandretti

Four Weeks to Fear LESS: Discovering and Dismantling Barriers to Peace
Copyrighted © 2023 Laura E. Sandretti
ISBN 9798853260788
First Edition

Four Weeks to Fear LESS: Discovering and Dismantling Barriers to Peace
by Laura E. Sandretti
Edited by Leslee Baron
Cover and interior design by Emmie Nosek

All Rights Reserved. Written permission must be secured from the author to reproduce any part of this book, except for brief quotations in critical reviews or articles. This book or parts thereof may not be reproduced in any form, or transmitted in any form by any means – electronic, mechanical, photocopy, recording, or otherwise – without prior written permission of the author.

To contact the author, or find out more about Laura and her ministry,
please visit laurasandretti.com.

All Scripture quotations, unless otherwise indicated, are taken from the Holy Bible, New International Version®, NIV®. Copyright © 1973, 1978, 1984, 2011 by Biblica, Inc.™

The author has made every effort to ensure that the information within this book was accurate at the time of publication. The author does not assume and hereby disclaims any liability to any party for any loss, damage, or disruption caused by errors or omissions, whether such errors or omissions result from accident, negligence, or any other cause.

Disclaimer

The author is not a therapist or licensed counselor. This book is not intended to replace medical, clinical, or professional advice, diagnosis, or medical intervention. *Four Weeks to Fear LESS* is designed to supplement, not replace, the reader's connectedness with Christ through prayer and reading the Bible.

Some of the content may be triggers for those who have struggled with anxiety attacks or other trauma and is intended for readers seventeen and up. Please contact a professional if you are struggling with mental health trauma or call 9-8-8 if you are experiencing suicidal thoughts.

To Hannah, Casey, Faithe, and Polo.

Thank you for being my amazing children.
I believe God redeems everything;
our struggles, fears, and failures are never wasted.

Because you believe in Jesus' death and resurrection,
I pray you will always remember God calls you
His righteous, forgiven, complete, and equipped child.

And that is who you are.

As Polo says,
"Believe it!"

Mom

TABLE OF CONTENTS

Introduction 12

Part One Discovering Barriers to Peace 15
Day One Expect More 16
Day Two Get Concrete 18
Day Three Look for Bricks 20
Day Four Talk to Yourself 22
Day Five Think Small 24
Day Six Don't Blame Yourself 26
Day Seven Widen Your Lens 28
Day Eight Be Honest 30
Day Nine Listen to Your Head 32
Day Ten Open a Box 34

Part Two Dismantling Barriers to Peace 37
Day Eleven Ask What Now? 38
Day Twelve Trust Slow is Sweet 40
Day Thirteen Open Your Eyes 42
Day Fourteen Think of a Child 44
Day Fifteen Look for Light 46
Day Sixteen Mind Your Mirror 48
Day Seventeen Fill-in-the-Blank 50
Day Eighteen Wrestle 54
Day Nineteen Read Context 56
Day Twenty See Your Humanness 58
Day Twenty-One Know the Real Jesus 60
Day Twenty-Two Remember a Rescue 62
Day Twenty-Three Find a Friend 64
Day Twenty-Four Watch the News 66
Day Twenty-Five Make a List 68
Day Twenty-Six Get New Glasses 70
Day Twenty-Seven Trust Redemption 72
Day Twenty-Eight Repeat 74

Bibliography 76
Resources 79
About the Author 81

INTRODUCTION
TIPS Before You Begin

1. Request

There isn't a book in the world that can make us fearless. It is impossible to live without any fear, at least on this side of heaven, but we can cooperate with the Spirit in experiencing more peace to fear less. The best way to do that is to cultivate our relationship with Jesus through prayer and time in His Word, so ask the Lord to help you receive His love and peace each day before you read.

2. Read

Each day contains a short reading to help you journal (or draw) your responses more clearly and meaningfully. Please read each introduction because, like a road map, it will help you get where you're trying to go!

3. Resist

Although you can take longer than one day to complete each reading and response, try to avoid doing more than one day at a time to allow yourself time to deeply and thoughtfully pray about and process each suggestion.

4. Don't Roll (your eyes)

"The Fear LESS Facts" at the bottom of each page might sound like something your mom would tell you to help you worry less. However, they are insights we often overlook that can help in our battles with anxiety. So please give them a little attention!

5. Reach for LESS

The goal for the next four weeks is to fear less, not to become fearless. Frequently reminding yourself of that will help you with the next two "R's"!

6. Remain

Each day's reading includes "Something to Do" to help you fear less. Don't give up if the activities don't seem to be working at first. Stick with it. The first half of the book is about discovering fears, and the second is about dismantling them. Reading until the end of the book is critical.

7. Realize More

The beautiful part of everyone's journey to fear less is that God always has more peace for us. Knowing this has allowed me to write this book, even though I still struggle with anxiety. God has more freedom from anxiety for me, and for you. The more we practice receiving Jesus' love and grace, the more we will feel God's peace. It is my prayer that this book is just the beginning of God's "more" for you.

*"The greatest competitor of devotion to Jesus is service to Him.
It is never 'Do, do' with the Lord, but 'Be, be' and He will 'do' through you.
The only way to keep true to God is by a steady persistent refusal
to be interested in Christian work and to be
interested alone in Jesus Christ."*

Oswald Chambers

PART ONE

Discovering Barriers to Peace

*"I say to God my Rock,
'Why have You forgotten me?
Why must I go about mourning,
oppressed by the enemy?'*

*Why, my soul, are you downcast?
Why so disturbed within me?
Put your hope in God,
for I will yet praise Him,
my Savior and my God."*

Psalm 42:9 & 11

Day One

Me Christmas Day

EXPECT MORE

"But hope that is seen is no hope at all. Who hopes for what they already have? But if we hope for what we do not yet have, we wait for it patiently."
Romans 8:24b & 25

When I tell women, whether they're twenty-one or fifty-one, that the Lord freed me over the span of thirty years from the bondage of panic attacks and the prison of crippling fear, they always ask me the same thing: "What did you do?"

This book tries to answer that question and provides tangible things you can do to fear less. However, the title of this guided response journal is not "Four Weeks to Fearless." There isn't a book, psychiatrist, or formula that can make us fearless. Even Jesus experienced fear (Luke 22:42-44), and although I haven't had a panic attack in twenty years, I still battle anxiety. I worry about my kids daily. If someone doesn't text me back, I think about what I may have said or done to upset them. If I get a bad migraine, I wonder if I have a tumor.

Although I still wrestle with fear, God has helped me fear less. I don't check my children's locations daily like I used to. If someone is upset with me, I don't mentally replay the conversation as long or often as I once did. When I have a health issue, I don't frantically comb the internet for hours to see how long I have left to live. I'm no longer afraid of bees or flying—unless it's turbulent. I still don't love that. The Lord has helped me fear less as I've learned to trust Him more. I've experienced the Spirit's peace and protection as I've become more open to His activity. And you can too.

I know that sounds nice, but also maybe like that's not enough. What we really want to know is what we can do to fear less. The good news is there are things we can do to experience more of Christ's peace that helps us fear less.

Something to Do

God does not want you to live in a prison of fear, so much so that He sent Jesus to provide us peace no matter what comes our way in life (Psalm 85:8 and Isaiah 53:5). He wants and has equipped you to feel comfortable and confident around groups of people, driving on the freeway, or talking to that guy. Maybe you can't imagine any of those things ever happening. Maybe you picked this book up because you're desperate to stop feeling anxious, but you don't know if God will or can help you. I get it. I've been there.

When we don't know where to start and have lost hope, one way to begin is to make room in our minds for God's peace. Before we begin to discover barriers to peace, we need to practice expanding our imagination and regain hope that we can fear less.

Write or draw a time when something wonderfully unexpected happened. Did you receive an extraordinary gift? Did someone throw you a surprise party? Reflect on a time when you or someone you love was incredibly sick but recovered when all seemed lost. In other words, write about or draw something that left you pleasantly amazed. If you can't think of anything, describe or draw what your ideal day would look like.

FEAR LESS FACT: STUDIES HAVE SHOWN THAT "DANCE, PAINTING, OR CREATING MUSIC ... CAN HELP PEOPLE WITH DEPRESSION, ANXIETY, AND STRESS."[1] TODAY, INSTEAD OF JUMPING ON TIKTOK TO UNWIND, DRAW, SKETCH, OR JUST DANCE FOR THIRTY MINUTES (OR LONGER IF YOU HAVE TIME!).

Day Two

On my phone since 1999

GET CONCRETE

"When Jesus saw him lying there and learned that he had been in this condition for a long time, He asked him, 'Do you want to get well?'"
John 5:6

My husband and I recently started a devotional about using our phones less. I hate how often I pick up my phone to text someone, only to realize twenty minutes later that I bought three things, watched two dog videos, and never texted the person I'd intended to. My subconscious expectation was that the devotional would help me quit being on my phone so much, but my screen time had increased less than a week into the study.

Like my expectation that the devotional would greatly reduce my time on my phone, our expectation is not to fear less. Our hope is that we will immediately and altogether stop being afraid. We do not intentionally establish these unrealistic desires, but subconsciously that's what we want. We want to live a stress-free, worry-free, problem-free life. That's what I want, anyway. My head knows that's unrealistic, but since even minor inconveniences and disappointments frustrate me, I know it's what I expect.

The obvious question then becomes, *How?* How do we establish realistic expectations about how to fear less when panic attacks and anxiety are so consuming and frightening? How do we sit in our hatred of fear, without wishing the impossible – that we could be completely unafraid? What do we do?

Something To Do

Getting concrete, a.k.a. getting specific about our actual life and problems, is something we will talk about and practice repeatedly in this book. Why? Well, let's use my phone devotional example. Although I knew I was on my phone a lot, I was shocked when I saw that I was on it for over forty hours a week. A number is concrete. "A lot" is vague and unhelpful. Getting concrete wakes us up and helps us approach our struggles more practically and effectively.

Getting concrete also helps us separate truth from fiction. When I saw how much time I was on my phone I was embarrassed, especially because my husband's screen time was so much less than mine. However, when I looked at the breakdown of those forty hours, most of it was spent connecting with the eight women I disciple every week.

Specific and concrete information can also show us how quick we are to be unkind and unfair to ourselves. Comparing ourselves to others and demonizing our thoughts and actions makes us miss the grace Christ has for us, grace that helps us fear less. Much more about that later, but for now, let's practice getting concrete.

Where specifically do you want to fear less? That will probably be a difficult question if you're anxious about many things like me. But remember, God wants to free you from fears that rob you of living life more richly and abundantly (John 10:10).

On the concrete brick below, write down one thing you wish you could fear less. Do you want to quit having panic attacks? Are you a twenty-something that wishes you could decide on a career? Are you a mom who is afraid to let your children out of your sight? Are you tired of worrying about an active shooter being at the theater or mall?

Write down the fear you would most like to fear less, or write down several fears, but circle the one that robs you of the most emotional and mental energy.

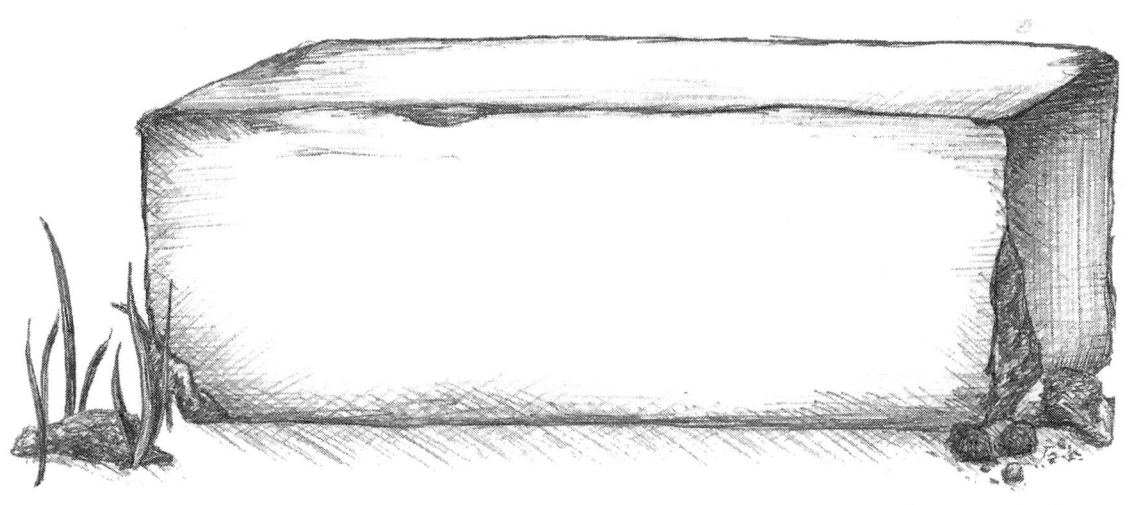

FEAR LESS FACT: "PURPOSEFUL DEEP BREATHING CAN PHYSICALLY CALM YOUR BODY DOWN IF YOU'RE FEELING STRESSED OR ANXIOUS."[2]
TAKE THREE DEEP, SLOW BREATHS BEFORE YOU EAT BREAKFAST, LUNCH, AND DINNER TODAY.

Day Three

Me, Luke, and Pop

LOOK FOR BRICKS

*"He will cover you with his feathers. He will shelter you with His wings.
His faithful promises are your armor and protection."*
Psalm 91:4 (NLT)

One of the biggest obstacles to peace is recognizing how dark, heavy, and all-consuming the weight of anxiety is. Yesterday you wrote down one of those concrete fears. You wrote it on a brick because we're going to use bricks as a visual to help us discover barriers to peace. Whenever we feel threatened by an everyday fear, real or imagined, we put up figurative bricks of protection to try and prevent more anxiety and distress. Identifying those bricks is going to help us get concrete and fear less.

I put up bricks, for example, every time I'd escape to my room when I had a panic attack or avoid watching the anxiety-inducing news. I put up more bricks when I'd use humor to hide my fears. In college, I put up new bricks by drinking and partying to deal with my anxiety. As an adult, I've put up bricks by keeping overly busy. Whenever we forgo or forget to invite the Lord into our fears and responses to those fears, we add bricks to a subconscious wall that gives us the perception of safety and control. We feel more insulated and protected behind our bricks of shyness, sarcasm, or isolation, but the truth is, we aren't.

In the coming days we are going to spend time paying attention to the protective brick walls we've constructed over the years. We are also going to get concrete about how thick those walls have become. We'll talk more about why that's important later, but for now, let's spend some time familiarizing ourselves with our bricks.

Something to Do

One distinct childhood memory I have was my family driving to Dairy Queen and my dad spotting a young man spraying graffiti on a building in our rural hometown. Despite the pleading of his horrified children from the back seat, my dad drove up to that building, jumped out of the car, and started chasing Rice Lake, Wisconsin's most hardened criminal. I learned at that moment that there were bad people in the world and that the world outside my house (and car) was unsafe.

One way to look for bricks and get concrete about how dense our walls are is to think back to times you were afraid and how you responded to those fears. Do you remember the first time you realized there were bad people or feeling afraid when you were home alone? Maybe, like me, you've experienced panic attacks and have tried to figure out what causes them and how to avoid them.

On the bricks below, write any fears you've had and a word or two about how you've responded to those fears. As you write, pray, and ask the Lord if there is anything else you could add to your brick pile. An eighteen-year-old woman I was discipling told me repeatedly that she couldn't remember what she was afraid of as a kid or when her fears started to feel debilitating. She struggled to get concrete, so we eventually decided to pray every day for two weeks. After that, she returned with over twenty memories of when she was afraid or had gotten in trouble (another big fear).

The Lord wants to help bring anything into the light that will help you fear less. As you pray, God may bring to your mind more fears you've had and how you've responded to them. Try to remember He does that because He loves and has more peace for you. Keep adding to the brick pile as you think of the times you were afraid and the ways you responded to those fears. You might be surprised how tall your walls are.

FEAR LESS FACT: SPEAKING OF DAIRY QUEEN, DID YOU KNOW THAT EATING SUGAR CAN CONTRIBUTE TO ANXIETY?[3] I'VE FOUND THAT RATHER THAN AVOIDING UNHEALTHY FOOD ALTOGETHER, ADDING A FEW HEALTHY SNACKS INSTEAD HELPS ME EAT BETTER AND FEEL LESS DEPRIVED. TODAY, EAT ONE OF YOUR FAVORITE VEGETABLES.

Day Four

Five-year-old me

TALK TO YOURSELF

"Finally brothers and sisters, whatever is true, whatever is noble, whatever is right, whatever is pure, whatever is lovely, whatever is admirable—if anything is excellent or praiseworthy—think about such things."
Philippians 4:8b

I was about five years old the first time it happened. I was in my driveway and suddenly felt like I needed to run or hide. My stomach churned, and my heart raced. I was overtaken by a sick, anxious feeling that consumed my mind, body, and soul. Little did I know that would be the first of hundreds of times that spirit of fear and dread would overwhelm me.

Although I was terrified by what was happening, I didn't tell anyone about my recurring episodes of debilitating anxiety until I was an adult. It was difficult to put what I was feeling into words, especially since people didn't talk about mental health issues when I was growing up.

I had no clue there was a name for what I was going through or that other people also had "panic attacks," as I later learned they were called. There weren't many people that I talked to about my panic attacks, but when I found someone I felt comfortable sharing with, they usually asked me what caused them. That question became a source of frustration and confusion for me since I didn't know what caused them or how to stop them.

There were other things that I kept to myself too; feelings I think my young brain was afraid to share, thought no one would understand, or worse yet, that I would get in trouble for. In addition to the panic attacks, there were many other fears and anxieties I struggled with alone because I thought I was alone in experiencing them. That isolation created more bricks to try to protect myself. Even five decades later, the voice in the back of my head still tries to convince me I'm weird or different and the only one who struggles with hard things.

One of the first ways we can start to fear less is to remind ourselves often that we are not alone. We are not the only one afraid of graduating, clowns, or dying. We are not strange because we don't like crowds or loud noises. In our minds, we know we aren't alone. Still, in our hearts, the enemy will attack and accuse us (Revelation 12:10b). Unfortunately, we rarely default to thinking true and helpful things about our fears and ourselves. But it doesn't have to stay this way.

Something To Do

Do you have fears you haven't shared with anyone? Are there things you struggle with alone because you think others won't understand or might get upset? Do you keep things to yourself, so people won't think something is wrong, or worse, wrong with you? Write them on the bricks below.

Why? Because part of examining our expectations is bringing our fears into proper perspective. The more we've hidden things in the dark and believed the lie that we are alone in them, the harder it will be to fear less. So, let's practice bringing fears we've kept secret into the light by simply writing them below. If you can, share them with someone you trust.

As you add to your brick pile, remind yourself you are not alone in these fears. King Solomon said, "there is nothing new under the sun" (Ecclesiastes 1:9b). You aren't the first person to be afraid of butterflies (one of my kids' friends is too), and you will not be the last. If you struggle to think of what to write or can't bring yourself to write down those struggles, that's okay. Ask the Lord to help you. Although this is a four-week journal, if you need four months to work through it, take that time.

FEAR LESS FACT: JULIANNE HOLT-LUNSTAD, PH.D., A PROFESSOR OF PSYCHOLOGY AND NEUROSCIENCE AT BRIGHAM YOUNG UNIVERSITY, FOUND THAT A "LACK OF SOCIAL CONNECTION HEIGHTENS HEALTH RISKS AS MUCH AS SMOKING 15 CIGARETTES A DAY OR HAVING ALCOHOL USE DISORDER" AND "LONELINESS AND SOCIAL ISOLATION ARE TWICE AS HARMFUL TO PHYSICAL AND MENTAL HEALTH AS OBESITY."[4] MAKE A COFFEE DATE WITH A FRIEND OR FAMILY MEMBER TODAY.

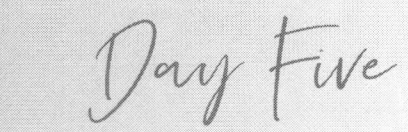

First day of school

THINK SMALL

"Or suppose a woman has ten silver coins and loses one. Doesn't she light a lamp, sweep the house and search carefully until she finds it?"
Luke 15:8

Every time you've had a panic attack or you've experienced any significant fear, you've put up a brick, and the same is true for me. However, we also put bricks up when we are afraid or hurt by the hundreds of seemingly small things that happen every day.

For example, when I was little, a huge snapping turtle clamped its jaw onto a shovel my dad was using to scoop him up. After that, I put up a brick by staying inside to avoid turtles. I remember another incident when I was putting on my favorite corduroy jacket when a hot, stinging sensation penetrated my arm. My dad, realizing a bee was stinging me, helped me get my coat off, then started relentlessly pummeling my innocent sherpa lined jacket against the ground with a violence never before witnessed by my young eyes. Consequently, my fear of bees followed me well into adulthood.

The list of seemingly insignificant things that made my palms sweat, stomach churn, and ears get hot was extensive: the first day of kindergarten; moving to a new school (in second, seventh, and twelfth grade); talking about Japan in social studies in my all-white school where my brothers and I were the only Asians; taking timed standardized tests where the oval had to be filled in exactly this way but not that way; applying for jobs; taking my driver's test; and getting my first (second, third, fifth…) speeding ticket(s). Even fears that seem less significant teach us to put up bricks and add to the burden and weight of living with constant anxiety.

Something To Do

It's time to add more bricks to your wall. Today, add the seemingly small and insignificant things you were or still are afraid of (like my fear of swallowing pills that I struggled with well into high school or my hatred of scenes filmed in the ocean). You don't need to explain them or write down more than a word or two. All you are doing is continuing to pay attention to how thick and tall your walls are.

Why? Because as the Lord helps us to fear less, we will get frustrated that we're still having panic attacks. We will still be afraid, and we'll probably be angry that it doesn't seem like anything is happening. We might question if God cares about us or if faith in Jesus makes a difference.

However, being able to look back at our brick walls will remind us we did not become fearful overnight. Seeing the magnitude of our walls will help us remember that our fears and how we've coped with them did not appear quickly. They will help us not get as frustrated and discouraged when they also don't go away quickly.

In the bricks below, write some day-to-day things you fear or have been afraid of in the past.

FEAR LESS FACT: PSALM 139:13 & 14 SAYS, "FOR YOU CREATED MY INMOST BEING; YOU KNIT ME TOGETHER IN MY MOTHER'S WOMB. I PRAISE YOU BECAUSE I AM FEARFULLY AND WONDERFULLY MADE; YOUR WORKS ARE WONDERFUL." POST THIS PASSAGE ON YOUR BATHROOM MIRROR TODAY. ASK GOD TO HELP YOU BELIEVE YOU ARE FEARFULLY AND WONDERFULLY MADE BY HIM WHEN YOU LOOK AT YOUR REFLECTION.

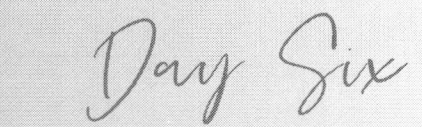

Me, Luke, and Ken

DON'T BLAME YOURSELF

*"Therefore there is now no condemnation
at all for those who are in Christ Jesus."*
Romans 8:1 (NASB)

When I was five, ten, sixteen, and even into adulthood, I tried making deals with God. I thought if I promised to stop hitting my two brothers or being so sarcastic, the Lord would stop my anxiety or get that cute guy to ask me out. Of course, it didn't take long to realize that bartering with the God of the universe didn't result in either one of us holding up our end of the bargain. I couldn't consistently do what I'd promised, and similarly, I didn't get whatever I asked the Lord for, including an end to my panic attacks. This made me wonder if something I was doing or failing to do was the reason that spirit of dread and darkness overtook me.

Since the Lord didn't seem to answer my prayers to remove my panic attacks, I concluded it was because I hadn't done what I promised Him I'd do. And perhaps the only thing worse than fear and panic attacks themselves, is the sense that we have control over our panic attacks but that we aren't good enough or don't have a strong enough faith to stop them. Although my brain knows that isn't true according to the Bible (2 Corinthians 12:7-9 and John 9:1-3), I still must remind myself that fear isn't punishment from the Lord. I need to constantly remember that Christ took care of all my shortcomings on the cross and that He never accuses me (Psalm 103:8-12).

Something to Do

What have you tried in your battles against fear? Have you, like me, bartered with and begged God for help only to feel no relief? Have you tried sleeping in or isolating yourself in your room? Have you talked to a friend or counselor, but lost hope that you'll ever stop feeling anxious?

On the bricks below, describe in a word or two how you've tried to cope with and prevent your fears. The things we've used to protect ourselves from anxiety aren't necessarily bad in and of themselves, but I've found that most of the ways I've tried to deal with my fears have been exhausting and ineffective. So, although our coping mechanisms aren't necessarily wrong (though some of mine were), the Lord wants to free us from dealing with our fears in ways that lead to fatigue and bondage. Remember this as you write on the bricks below the ways you've coped with and tried stopping your anxiety.

FEAR LESS FACT: "LAUGHTER AND HUMOR INTERVENTIONS ARE EFFECTIVE IN RELIEVING DEPRESSION, ANXIETY, AND IMPROVE SLEEP QUALITY IN ADULTS."[5] TRY WATCHING A FUNNY TV SHOW SOMETIME TODAY AND ENJOY THE BENEFITS OF A GOOD LAUGH.

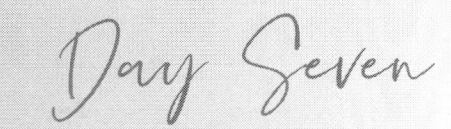

Day Seven

Me and Luke

WIDEN YOUR LENS

> *"When he first arrived, he ate with the Gentile believers, who were not circumcised. But afterward, when some friends of James came, Peter wouldn't eat with the Gentiles anymore. He was afraid of criticism from these people who insisted on the necessity of circumcision who were not circumcised."*
> Galatians 2:12 (NLT)

So far, we have mostly discussed fears associated with things—things like turtles and bees, or my longtime fear of tornadoes. But the fear of things and the bricks we've put up to protect ourselves from those things aren't the only barriers to overcome before we can fear less. If we widen the lens through which we think about our anxieties, we'll see that people are scary, too, and perhaps one of our biggest fears of all.

The first time I remember being afraid of people was when I was about four years old. I overheard my parents talking about selling their car because according to my father, and I quote, "It's a piece of junk." Sometime after overhearing that conversation, I was playing outside with my older brother, Luke, when I noticed two people thoroughly and thoughtfully inspecting said vehicle. When I proudly informed them, "My dad said this car is a piece of junk," Luke looked at me in horror and said the four words I feared most, "I'm telling on you!"

I had no idea why he was telling on me, but I could tell by his terrified expression and lightning speed that I was in for it. Terrified and confused, I ran to my room and crawled under my bed. Although I've joked about that story many times, I realized recently that this story wasn't a funny or isolated occurrence. Well into adulthood, I tried to avoid getting in trouble like I did when I was four. Over the years, I've put up many, many bricks to try to prevent being corrected or disciplined. Those bricks didn't protect me from anything, but they were walls I constructed, nevertheless.

Something To Do

Let's widen our lens, and our brick pile while we're at it. To get started, consider how you'd respond in the following scenarios. You get called to the school office or to see your boss;

what is your immediate reaction? Are you afraid you've done something wrong? How do you feel going through the security area at the airport? Stressed? What feelings arise when you think about talking to someone you don't know or having to make an appointment over the phone? Nervousness? Anxiety?

Over the next twenty-four hours, mark a brick whenever you catch yourself dwelling on other people's feelings or what they're thinking. If you're wondering if someone was upset with you or if you overexplained something to ensure they knew you had good intentions, color another brick. If you put off having a conversation with someone or changed your outfit ten times before going out last night…well, you get the idea.

Resist the urge to fix, explain, or justify what you notice. Try merely to add to your brick pile by paying attention to when you are trying to impress, please, or keep others from correcting you. Be kind to yourself as you pay attention to your fears surrounding people. Ask the Lord to help you not feel ashamed or embarrassed as you add to your brick wall below. His Word says He's on your side and cares about you (Deuteronomy 31:8). You are not alone in these fears!

FEAR LESS FACT: PRACTICING COMPASSION AND HELPING OTHERS CAN HELP REDUCE ANXIETY AND DEPRESSION.[6] BEFORE BED, PRAY FOR SOMEONE YOU KNOW WHO IS DEALING WITH A DIFFICULT SITUATION OR RELATIONSHIP.

Day Eight

My brother, Kenny

BE HONEST

"Jesus went out as usual to the Mount of Olives... And being in anguish, he prayed more earnestly, and his sweat was like drops of blood falling to the ground."
Luke 22:39a & 44

When I was younger, one of the only things that consistently seemed to trigger a panic attack was my fear of dying. As a child, I thought everyone died in age order. When I was the youngest child, I worried my dad would die first, followed by my mom and older brother. The thought of being without my family added to the horror of my anxieties surrounding death. Fortunately, as luck would have it, when I was seven, my little brother Kenny was born. If my theory about dying in age order held up, I'd no longer be the last one from my family on Earth! I was so happy when Kenny was born!

The fear of death and being alone because of death impacted me frequently. Once, I saw a scene on TV where someone pulled a chain to turn on a light, and the room blew up. That prompted an instant panic attack. I recall the first funeral I went to and how sad everyone was. After the funeral experience, whenever my parents got home late, I'd be filled with terror thinking they had gotten in an accident. Or when my brother had to go to the hospital once with severe stomach pains, I worried he'd never come home. Anticipating worst-case scenarios, I suppose, were more bricks to try to plan for and protect myself from my fears.

When I got older, I learned that Jesus Christ died to forgive me of my sins and give me eternal life, so I didn't have to fear death. But I still did. And because I did, I was not only scared to die, I felt guilty for being afraid. I didn't think "good Christians" were supposed to fear death, and because no one talked about it, I thought I was the only Christian who did. Although God isn't disappointed or angry with us because we're afraid to die (again, remember that Jesus was, too), this was my fear.

Being honest about the things we're afraid of is a way to cooperate with the Spirit. If we blindly *should* ourselves to death, like saying, "You *should* not be afraid of dying" or

"Good Christians *should* look forward to being with Jesus," we will continue to be afraid. Additionally, if we aren't honest with those struggles, we will doubt the Lord's love and compassion, the very thing that will help us most in learning to fear less. We will talk more about that later, but for now, try to remember and trust that God meets us with love, grace, and compassion where we really are, not where we think we should be. We can't "renew our minds" (Romans 12:2) if we avoid acknowledging the difficult thoughts going on in them!

Something to Do

Can you relate to my fear of death? Were you, or are you, sometimes preoccupied with thoughts of losing a family member or being alone? Do you remember the first funeral you attended? Let's get concrete by bringing our past and present fears into the light. Becoming aware of our brick walls helps us discover barriers to peace, be kinder to ourselves, and understand why we need the Lord's help.

Write in a few words on the bricks below any thoughts, memories, or fears you have or had regarding death. This may be a trigger for you as it was for me. If you need to work through this with a therapist or pastor, do not hesitate to do so.

FEAR LESS FACT: SOMETIMES, WE HAVE DIFFICULTY LETTING GO OF THE FEARS WE'VE ASKED GOD TO TAKE AWAY. TODAY, WRITE DOWN WHAT YOU'RE ANXIOUS OR WORRIED ABOUT ON SOME ROCKS, LEAVES, OR SMALL PIECES OF PAPER. THEN, THROW THE ROCKS IN A POND OR RIVER, OR IF YOU USED LEAVES OR PAPER, WATCH THEM BLOW AWAY IN THE WIND. THIS ACTIVITY HAS HELPED SEVERAL WOMEN I DISCIPLE SURRENDER THEIR FEARS MORE FULLY TO THE LORD.

Day Nine

A humbling photo of me getting blocked

LISTEN TO YOUR HEAD

"Such love has no fear, because perfect love expels all fear. If we are afraid, it is for fear of punishment, and this shows that we have not fully experienced his perfect love."
I John 4:18 (NLT)

A young woman I'm discipling struggles to believe God loves her. She thinks He is upset with her and is always trying to teach her a lesson. Although she's been a Christian her entire life and knows what the Bible says about God's love for her, she doesn't feel it. She also struggles with guilt and feels bad about herself because she still lives at home, doesn't have a full-time job, and isn't dating anyone. She feels like she's lazy and that there is something wrong with her.

One way to start to fear less is to pay attention to how you talk about yourself. Do you highlight your flaws and mistakes? Do you make jokes about being unattractive or a bad cook? Perhaps you call yourself an idiot or stupid when you do or say something embarrassing. Listening to what we say about ourselves when we mess up is a good indicator of how we think God sees us. Paying attention to when we talk about ourselves in ways God never would helps us get concrete.

Why? 1 John 4:18a says, "There is no fear in love. But perfect love drives out fear because fear has to do with punishment." If we think God is disappointed with us and will likely punish us, we will struggle to fear less. Most of us would say we trust that Jesus died for all of our sins (Colossians 2:13b) so we don't have to fear being punished when we mess up. However, paying attention to when we condemn and criticize ourselves will help us realize that we often don't fully believe or accept Christ's forgiveness.

Something to Do

We are going to add some more bricks to our brick pile by paying attention to how we talk to ourselves when we skip church, swear at bad drivers, or drink too much after finals. How we see ourselves when we fail reflects how we believe God sees us. What does your head call you when you get into an argument with your dad (again) or gossip about your co-workers?

How we talk to ourselves when we mess up isn't the only way to discover our view of God. Suppose we are overly excited by getting an 'A' or are constantly seeking out compliments and approval from others. In that case, we probably think God is happier with us when we're doing well or being successful, which isn't true according to the Bible (Isaiah 64:6). Being consumed with accolades and achievements also adds to our wall.

Why? Because as exhausting as it feels to beat ourselves up when we fail, it's equally draining to get our worth from the things we do well, and the compliments we receive. It's tiring because no matter how much good we do, if someone else does those things better, it will make us wonder if we're good (pretty, smart, etc.) enough. We feel hurt and dismissed when we aren't thanked or don't feel seen; all of this is grounded in fear, and it's exhausting.

On the bricks below, write down any thoughts you have about yourself, good or bad. Try to avoid justifying or feeling ashamed about what you write. In the second part of the book, we will talk about what to do with those thoughts. Until then, remember that because of Jesus, you are loved by God, whether you are partying or praying. (See Psalm 103:8-12 again if you don't believe me.)

FEAR LESS FACT: A 2008 STUDY FROM THE JOURNAL OF ANXIETY DISORDERS FOUND "THAT IN PEOPLE WHO WERE SOCIALLY AWKWARD, THEIR PERFORMANCE WAS GENERALLY WORSE IN THEIR HEADS COMPARED TO WHAT ACTUALLY OCCURRED."[7] TODAY, CALL A FRIEND WHO MAKES YOU SMILE AND ENJOY THE BENEFITS OF SOCIALIZING TO FEAR LESS.

Day Ten

Hiding behind a smile in 1987

OPEN A BOX

"The light shines in the darkness, and the darkness has not overcome it."
John 1:5

In my late forties, I joined a discipleship group where I shared for one of the first times a secret I'd had since I was young. When I was very small, I was molested. In the seventies, there wasn't much talk about "stranger danger" (or apparently much of anything related to most of my childhood trauma), so besides telling my mom and husband, this wasn't a memory I'd brought into the light until that small group of women.

When I shared this with my discipleship group, I remember saying that I didn't think what had happened to me when I was little had impacted me very much. I felt like it was a memory I had buried in a box in my mind that I didn't think about or open. It was something that I rarely thought about, but in hindsight, it was a significant part of why I struggled with fear from such an early age and something that would have been helpful to process with a pastor or therapist.

I know many women have stories like mine and feel that the "box" that holds their secret isn't significant, or that opening it won't change what happened. I would encourage you, however, if you have a story of sexual abuse or trauma, to be sure and process what happened with a parent or Christian counselor if you haven't before. Talking about the difficult and painful stories we've buried deeply for years or even decades can help ensure those boxes don't rot or get relocated without our permission.

Something to Do

Do you have a box like mine? Do you have a difficult memory that you don't think about very often? Memories hidden in secret boxes can have authority in our lives when we keep them in the dark, but we can regain that power when we bring them into the light.

It can be therapeutic and clarifying to share the unopened things lurking in our heads because significant memories can impact and shape our thoughts, fears, and the walls we've put up.

If you are comfortable and it pertains to you, write down any difficult memories that come to mind. One young woman I disciple told me her family pretended to leave her at a park when she was young because she didn't listen when it was time to go. That abandonment and rejection shaped her in an unhealthy way for twenty-five years. Another woman recalled a painful memory she'd buried deeply in her box; her siblings laughing at her when she got hit in the face with a shovel. That humiliation and pain made it hard for her to trust others. Another woman had sexual trauma like mine that overwhelmed her with guilt and shame.

If you aren't sure if you have any difficult memories hidden in a box, ask the Lord about it this week and write down or draw anything that comes to mind. If what you write about or uncover feels overwhelming and hard to process, reach out to a health professional or one of the resources in the back of this book for help.

FEAR LESS FACT: "EVIDENCE THAT ANXIETY DISORDERS ARE ASSOCIATED WITH GENERAL MEDICAL CONDITIONS IS GROWING."[8] A YOUNG WOMAN I WAS DISCIPLING STRUGGLED WITH ANXIETY AND FATIGUE. WHEN I ENCOURAGED HER TO SEE HER DOCTOR, SHE DISCOVERED SHE HAD A THYROID CONDITION. IF YOU HAVEN'T HAD A PHYSICAL IN A WHILE, TALK TO YOUR PARENT AND/OR SCHEDULE ONE SOON.

"The Christian life, from one angle, is the long journey of letting our natural assumptions about who God is, over many decades, fall away, being slowly replaced with God's own insistence on who He is. This is hard work.
It takes lots of sermons and a lot of suffering to believe that
God's deepest heart is "merciful and gracious, slow to anger."[9]

Dane Ortlund, Gentle and Lowly

PART TWO

Dismantling Barriers to Peace

*"And may you have the power
to understand, as all God's people
should, how wide, how long,
how high, and how deep his love is.
May you experience the love
of Christ, though it is too great to
understand fully. Then you will be made
complete with all the fullness of life
and power that comes from God."*

Ephesians 3:18-19 (NLT)

Day Eleven

My courageous kids

ASK: WHAT NOW?

"…but I focus on this one thing: Forgetting the past and looking forward to what lies ahead, I press on to reach the end of the race and receive the heavenly prize for which God, through Christ Jesus, is calling us."
Philippians 3:13b & 14 (NLT)

For many years I thought and prayed about, *Why?* Why was I so fearful? Why did and do I, at times, still default to assuming the worst and darkest outcomes? (Just today, a horrific and graphic image of something happening to a loved one popped into my head. You are not alone in those quiet and terrorizing thoughts that periodically surface out of nowhere.) Why did God allow me to be so fear-filled?

Asking *Why?* isn't bad. Doing so helps us get concrete. *Why?* helps us see and understand our brick walls and how they got so high and dense. However, at some point, the expense of my time and mental energy in asking why began to outweigh its benefits. Eventually, the Holy Spirit helped me realize that there was another important question that would help me move from discovering barriers to peace to dismantling them. That question is, "What now?"

When we move from asking *Why?* to *What now?*, we don't abandon the reasons we fear people and their criticism. Asking *What now?* doesn't diminish the hurt our boxes have caused or the fears we can't seem to escape. However, asking *What now?* can help us dismantle our walls of false protection. It can allow us to cooperate with the Spirit in moving closer to God's desire for us to fear less.

Something To Do

Have you ever thought about what it would look like if that fear you identified on Day Two lost some of its power? How would it feel to make a decision without second-guessing yourself? What would your relationship with that family member look like if you weren't afraid of being corrected or criticized? How freeing would it be if you weren't so worried about what people might talk to you about at that party next week?

In a few words or drawings describe how a specific anxiety in your life might look differently as you ask, *What now?* Begin to dream and expand your imagination for life beyond just asking why of your fears. The Lord has so much more for you as you begin to fear less.

FEAR LESS FACT: "STRETCHING HAS BEEN SHOWN TO INCREASE SEROTONIN LEVELS — I.E., THE HORMONE THAT HELPS STABILIZE OUR MOOD, REDUCE STRESS, AND OVERALL MAKES US FEEL GOOD — WHICH CAUSES A DECREASE IN DEPRESSION AND ANXIETY."[10] TAKE FIVE MINUTES WHILE YOU'RE WATCHING TV OR WAITING FOR DINNER TO STRETCH!

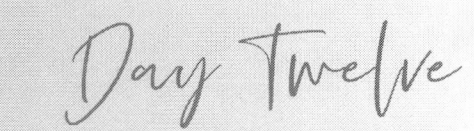

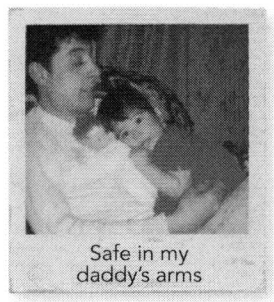

Safe in my daddy's arms

TRUST SLOW IS SWEET

"For he does not willingly bring affliction or grief to anyone."
Lamentations 3:33

There were many times over the past fifty-three years that I felt robbed of time, joy, and the ability to be present with loved ones because of my anxiety. Often, I felt frustrated and confused because it felt like the Lord wasn't helping me, or if He was, it seemed to be taking forever. However, as I started to ask, *What now?*, more often, I began to realize that what felt like God's slowness in dismantling my brick wall was a demonstration of His love and grace.

How? How could the slowness of God in removing that horrific feeling of dread and fear that I'd battled for so long possibly be His goodness? How could so much suffering possibly be something a good Father would allow His child to endure? Well, I learned that the answer wasn't so much about God as it was about me and my brick walls.

It may not feel like it, but God is merciful when He seems to be working at a turtle's pace in making our fears go away. How? Because we feel safe behind our brick walls. If the Lord answered our prayers all at once like we think we want, it would feel like someone taking a wrecking ball to the wall we've painstakingly and artfully constructed to protect ourselves.

Although we want our panic attacks and nagging anxiety to go away immediately and permanently, God's love and protection sweetly and slowly dismantle our walls, one brick at a time. The more we begin to trust Him and His love to meet us in our real problems, the more we will trust Him to lovingly remove each brick and gradually dismantle our barriers to peace.

Something To Do

In the next chapter, we will talk more about God's slowness and how that helps us fear less. For now, describe or draw a picture of yourself hiding behind your wall of fear and coping mechanisms.

Then describe or draw where Jesus is.

I'm guessing you've never thought about where Jesus is. Thinking about where Jesus is in relation to us, our fears, and other difficult things in our lives can help make our beliefs about Him more concrete and help us fear less.

When I gave this assignment to one woman, she drew Jesus far away from her, looking in the opposite direction from where she was. Another young woman drew God "all around" with blue squiggly lines. When I imagined where Jesus was when I was hiding under the bed after the "This car is a piece of junk" comment, I thought that Jesus would probably be on His knees, gently coaxing me out from under the bed and onto His lap. I also imagined my parents and brother knocking on the door of my room, but Jesus wouldn't let anyone come in or near me. I was safe in His arms.

I pray that as you dare to wonder about Christ's heart for you, that you find it's more beautiful than you could ever have imagined. If you realize that you think Jesus is distant or indifferent, that's okay. Your head probably knows that isn't what the Bible says about Jesus, but realizing your heart believes differently is a chance to pray and ask the Lord for help seeing Him differently. (If you'd prefer, feel free to journal your thoughts instead of drawing them.)

FEAR LESS FACT: "SONGS ALLOW YOU, AND THOSE AROUND YOU, HELP TO CALM YOUR NERVOUS SYSTEM, RELAX AND HEAL YOUR SOUL."[11] LISTEN TO YOUR FAVORITE SONG BEFORE BED TONIGHT.

Day Thirteen

Me and Kim

OPEN YOUR EYES

"The LORD your God is in your midst, a mighty one who will save; he will rejoice over you with gladness; he will quiet you by his love; he will exult over you with loud singing."
Zephaniah 3:17 (ESV)

As we begin to let the Lord take one brick at a time out of the wall we've put up to try and shield ourselves from further fear and pain, our instinct will be to resist. Part of our brain will tell us that praying won't help and that God doesn't care because if He did, He'd help us. I've wrestled with those legitimate arguments in the past and sometimes still do at the ripe old age of fifty-three. However, the dangerous irony about this thinking is that until we begin to trust God's love and care more, we will not ask, *What now?* Until we trust He's on our side, we will not trust Him to remove a brick in our wall. But how do we trust God when we really don't trust Him sometimes?

The best way to begin to trust the Lord more and fear less is to remind ourselves repeatedly that God sees us as valuable regardless of what we do—good or bad—and regardless of our motives—good or dark. We think we know this, but if we open our eyes wider to see ourselves more clearly, we'll realize that the truth of how God sees us isn't easy for us to accept. For some reason, it is always easier to believe God's love and promises for other people than it is for us. Tomorrow we will practice expanding our imagination to help us experience God's love for us apart from what we do, where we go to school, or how awesome (or not awesome) we are. But for now, let's get concrete.

Something to Do

Describe your best friend or favorite human. What do you love about them? What are their best qualities? My friend Kim is kind, funny, and makes the world's best scones. She is humble and can fix or build anything. She also has an amazing giggle and is one of the most generous people I know.

Describe your favorite human below and write one sentence about why you love them.

___

Now describe yourself. What are your best qualities? What makes you an amazing human?

___

Which of those descriptions was easier for you to write? Was it easy to come up with glowing things to say about your mom or boyfriend, but did it take longer to write one or two nice things about yourself? Did you enjoy describing your friend but feel uncomfortable writing positive things about yourself?

We struggle to see ourselves as the Lord does, and because of that, we do not intuitively trust the labels God assigns us in the Bible. If you believe Jesus Christ died on a cross and was raised back to life, you are a big deal. More about that tomorrow.

Fear LESS Fact: "A world Journal of Psychology study found that drinking less than two glasses of water, instead of the recommended five glasses at day, doubles your risk for depression and anxiety."[12] Drink a glass of water before each meal today or set a timer on your phone to take a sip every fifteen minutes.

Day Fourteen

Carter

THINK OF A CHILD

"Jesus said, 'Let the little children come to me, and do not hinder them, for the kingdom of heaven belongs to such as these.'"
Matthew 19:14

Yesterday we talked about experiencing less fear by learning to receive how God sees us. It's hard, isn't it? Well, today we are going to expand our imagination and make more room for *What now?* We are going to try to get a picture of God's heart for us so we can trust Him to slowly dismantle our wall. It isn't enough to realize that we struggle to accept who the Bible says we are. We must figure out how to continually receive the identity God gives us in Scripture.

My daughter used to nanny a little boy named Carter. Carter rarely listened to directions or rules. He often lied to and annoyed his siblings. He frequently got in trouble at school and tried the patience of many. He exhausted me with his inability to take any breaks from talking or doing so with an inside voice. When we're together, I rarely sit down as Carter constantly wants to show me everything and begs me to chase and play with him.

Nonetheless, I love Carter. I love how he wants to play hide-and-seek, and it cracks me up how annoying he is to his big sister. I love his brutal honesty, and I must hide my laughter when he looks my daughter square in the eye and tells her that he did eat his cucumbers when they're right in front of him in plain sight.

Note that Carter cannot *do* anything for me. He doesn't have money or a job. Carter doesn't tell me I'm beautiful or intelligent. He doesn't care that I write books and speak to people. He doesn't care about the house I live in or the clothes I wear, and he never thanks me for visiting or playing with him. Although Carter often acts naughty, and our relationship is not filled with mutual encouragement or adoration, it's easy for me to see the good, funny, and amazing things about him.

My relationship with Carter reminds me of God's heart for all of us. We often disobey, ignore rules, and do annoying things, but God loves us. We can't give God something He doesn't already have, yet He loves simply being with us, and cares for us deeply. Because of Jesus' death on our behalf, God sees the good, funny, and amazing things about us. We know this abstractly, but deep down we don't.

Underneath all our anxieties and behind the walls we've built to hide and protect ourselves, the root of the problem is we don't deeply believe God loves the weak, annoying, and ugly parts of us. Deep down, we're afraid we'll get in trouble with God and people. There's also part of us that feels we deserve to be punished, even though we *think* that we believe Jesus died to forgive us of our failures and sins. But it doesn't have to stay this way.

Something To Do

Google a Bible verse about fear or about who God says you are in Him. Search until you find a verse that makes you a little teary or stirs something in your heart. Then write the verse on the *fallen* brick below. Read it out loud but try to avoid sounding like a robot. Read it like you'd say it to a small person you love. Read it with the passion and emotion you'd use to convince your best friend or little sister that they are loved.

That is God's heart for you. He's on your side and cheering you on to a deeper belief in His love for you. And remember that you're writing that verse on a fallen brick because that is what God's Word helps us do. It dismantles lies, one brick at a time, letting in His light that reminds us He is safe. Remember that the brick walls we've built up only give us the illusion of protection. It is only God's love that can protect us in a way our self-manufactured walls never can.

FEAR LESS FACT: "RECENT STUDIES HAVE NOTED A SIGNIFICANT UPTICK IN DEPRESSION AND SUICIDAL THOUGHTS OVER THE PAST SEVERAL YEARS FOR TEENS, ESPECIALLY THOSE WHO SPEND MULTIPLE HOURS A DAY USING SCREENS, AND ESPECIALLY GIRLS."[13] PUT YOUR PHONE SOMEWHERE OUT OF REACH TODAY SO YOU CAN TRY TO SPEND LESS TIME ON YOUR SCREEN.

Day Fifteen

Our cabin and cellar door

LOOK FOR LIGHT

"The unfolding of your words gives light; it gives understanding to the simple."
Psalm 119:130

Once, when my kids were very young, we were vacationing at our cabin when a tornado siren went off. Our cabin was old, so we had to go outside to get into our creepy cellar with dirt walls and spiders galore. Death by tornado seemed to be the only thing worse than sitting in that basement, so if the siren seemed legitimate, down we would go.

When we got the all-clear and returned upstairs, I still had lingering anxiety and unrest in my soul from the storm, whose black clouds were still ominously encircling our cabin. Finally, I said a quick prayer. It's funny how prayer is often the last thing we turn to in times of fear. I suppose, in some ways, worrying gives us the illusion of control. Praying and asking God, whom we can't see, to help us when we're desperate and have tried everything else can feel a little like rolling the dice. Add to that the weight of feeling undeserving of His help (since most of us feel that way, don't we?), and prayer feels desperate and weak.

But when I finally asked for the Lord's help, something caught the corner of my eye. On the fence outside our kitchen window, there was an incredibly bright but tiny spot of light. It was a brilliant orange color and glowed like an ember. I wasn't sure where the light was coming from, but eventually, I realized a tiny ray of sunlight had broken through all those ominous black clouds.

That little light gave me a glimpse of God's mercy. That small glowing dot made me feel like God not only heard my prayer but that He cared, and at that moment, a brick of anxiety fell from my wall.

He replaced that brick with a reminder that He is the God who sees me (Genesis 16:13b). Although His answers to my heart's cries don't usually happen that quickly or obviously, whenever He meets me in my real fears, I begin to trust His slowness and goodness in new ways.

Something To Do

Go for a walk today (preferably somewhere quiet and pretty) and leave your smartwatch, phone, and AirPods behind. Look at the clouds, the trees, and feel the wind on your face (hopefully, it isn't January in Wisconsin when you take your walk). Take some deep breaths, and if you want to pray, do so. If you want to sing, do it!

Most of all, try to look for the Lord in His creation around you. Romans 1:20-21 (NLT) says, "For ever since the world was created, people have seen the earth and sky. Through everything God made, they can clearly see his invisible qualities—his eternal power and divine nature. So they have no excuse for not knowing God."

This verse reminds us that nature helps us see God's light and know Him. Can you put into words the beauty of a sunrise or adequately explain the variety of colors of the leaves in October? The fact that we cannot, reminds us of the bigness and beauty and goodness of God.

When we practice looking for His beautiful and loving light, it will help us trust Him to dismantle our walls with His love, one brick at a time. On the fallen brick below, jot down any feelings you had or lovely things you noticed on your walk.

FEAR LESS FACT: "GETTING YOUR HEART RATE UP CHANGES BRAIN CHEMISTRY, INCREASING THE AVAILABILITY OF IMPORTANT ANTI-ANXIETY NEUROCHEMICALS, INCLUDING SEROTONIN, GAMMA AMINOBUTYRIC ACID (GABA), BRAIN-DERIVED NEUROTROPHIC FACTOR (BDNF), AND ENDOCANNABINOIDS"[14] (WHATEVER THOSE ARE!). AFTER YOU ADD TO YOUR BRICK WALL, DESTRESS BY WORKING OUT OR GOING FOR A WALK.

Day Sixteen

The people I worried most about

MIND YOUR MIRROR

"The Lord is compassionate and gracious, slow to anger, abounding in love."
Psalm 103:8

During the throes of one of my most anxious seasons of life, when I became a new mom, I heard a Bible verse that piqued my curiosity. I did not grow up reading the Bible, so I had never heard this passage that encompassed what I longed for my entire life. When I heard it at a moms group I was attending, I was intrigued and filled with hope listening to the peace that Philippians 4:6-7 promised:

"Do not be anxious about anything, but in every situation, by prayer and petition, with thanksgiving, present your requests to God. And the peace of God, which transcends all understanding, will guard your hearts and your minds in Christ Jesus."

However, somewhere along the way, I began to hear it with a tone. When I was struggling with anxiety or another panic attack, I would hear the Lord angrily and with great annoyance say, "Do not be anxious about anything!" I felt like He was rolling his eyes because I was *still* afraid. After all, I knew what the Lord had done for me and how much He loved me. I thought He must be frustrated that I couldn't seem to improve in fearing less.

Why? Because I wasn't reading the Bible as an invitation from a loving Father who wanted good for me. I was reading it like God was an impatient dictator who was waiting for me to make Him happy. I knew God didn't need me to make Him happy. Jesus' death already assures me that the Lord delights in me. I abstractly believed that "Even before He made the world, God loved us and chose us in Christ to be holy and without fault in his eyes" (Ephesians 1:4, NLT), but I didn't believe it deeply.

Something to Do

How do you think God views your fear and anxiety? Is He irritated and frustrated? Does He wish you'd get over it already? Or do you deeply trust what it says in Psalm 56:8 (NLT), "You keep track of all my sorrows. You have collected all my tears in your bottle. You have recorded each one in your book"?

We looked at Zephaniah 3:17 earlier: "The LORD your God is with you, he is mighty to save. He will take great delight in you, he will quiet you with his love, he will rejoice over you with singing." It sounds romantic and lovely, but we usually do not believe it. Why? Because it is not enough to recite Scripture if we don't trust that the One who wrote the Bible loves and cares about us. The more we are able to read His Word as an invitation from a loving Father, the more we will start to fear less.

Today, try reading Zephaniah 3:17 to yourself in the mirror but personalize it. Read it in the first person like this, "Laura, I'm with you and delight in you. I want to save you and quiet your fears with my love, and I rejoice over you with singing whether you're succeeding or failing. Can you start to trust that I love you and want that for you?"

As you read, listen for the sound of a brick falling and feel the warmth of God's light penetrating the space that brick once occupied.

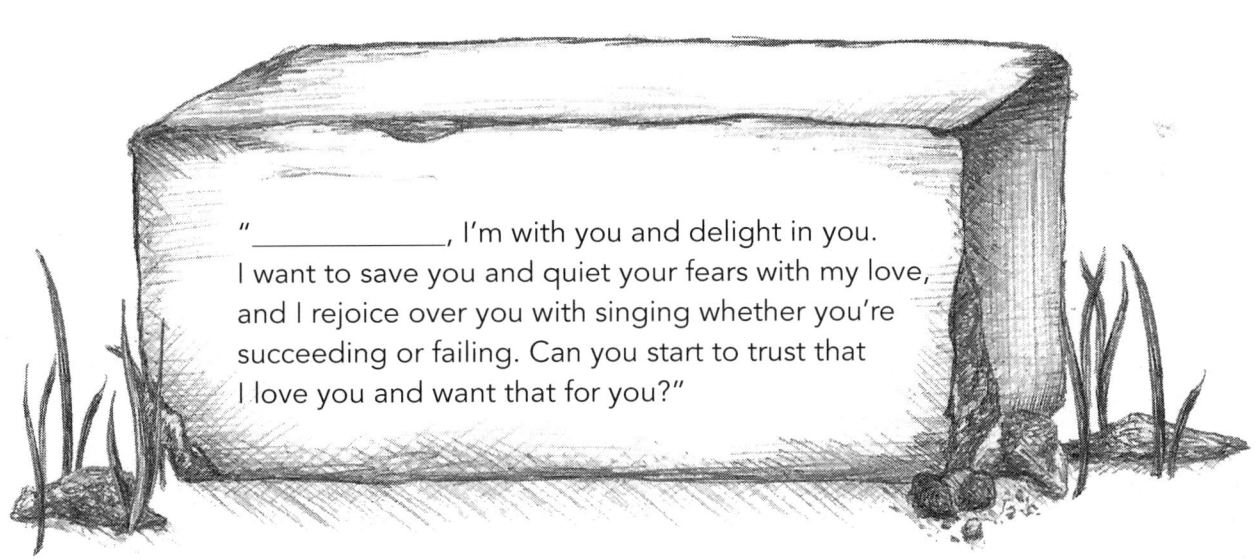

"_____, I'm with you and delight in you. I want to save you and quiet your fears with my love, and I rejoice over you with singing whether you're succeeding or failing. Can you start to trust that I love you and want that for you?"

FEAR LESS FACT: "AN EFFECTIVE ROUTINE CAN HELP REDUCE STRESS, WHICH CAN LEAD TO BETTER MENTAL HEALTH, MORE TIME TO RELAX, AND LESS ANXIETY."[15] IF YOU DON'T ALREADY HAVE A CALENDAR APP ON YOUR PHONE, DOWNLOAD ONE TODAY. IF YOU HAVE ONE AND DON'T USE IT, START BY PUTTING YOUR WORK OR EXAM SCHEDULE FOR THIS MONTH IN YOUR CALENDAR TODAY.

Day Seventeen

Fort Wilderness, WI, women's retreat

FILL-IN-THE-BLANK

"Your words were found, and I ate them, and your words became to me a joy and the delight of my heart, for I am called by your name, O Lord, God of hosts."
Jeremiah 15:16 (ESV)

I was speaking at a conference when a woman approached me. Her daughter's anxiety was so bad that the young girl did not want to go to school, and the mother didn't know what to do. I empathized with this poor woman since not only had I battled anxiety, but so have my children over the years. When the woman asked me how I had been freed from my panic attacks, I asked if she knew my go-to verse, Philippians 4:6-7. She not only knew it but recited it from memory. Yet she said that knowing the verse didn't seem to have made much of a difference.

Is it enough to know what God's Word says? Is memorizing and reciting verses like Philippians 4:6-7 enough to help us fear less? I believe it is because it was the most significant way I learned to fear less. However, as we've been talking about, until we trust the Lord's love for us more deeply, it may not feel like knowing God's Word is helping us fear less.

Part of the problem is that we say we have a "relationship with Jesus," but we don't often read the Bible as we would read a letter from a loved one. We instead treat Scripture like it's a behavior modification manual to teach us how to act and talk better. What lasting and healthy relationship consists only of one person constantly teaching the other how to behave differently?

A healthy relationship includes mutual encouragement, honesty, and compassion. God's Word is a way for us to know Him and His love, but if we don't trust God to help us with our real struggles and relationships, we will not read or rely on the Bible when we need it most. We won't obey the safeguards God gives us to protect us, either, which is another way to fear less. Until we learn to "combine" God's Word with our actual, concrete fears and anxieties, we won't trust Him more or fear less. How do we do that? I'm glad you asked.

Something to Do

One way to watch God's Word intersect with and impact our lives is to get concrete by doing, in part, what I suggested to that precious mom at the conference. I encouraged her to pray through Philippians 4:6-7 with her sweet little girl. We can "pray the Bible" by inserting specific problems and questions into His Word as we read it.

What do you wish would happen regarding something you're afraid of right now? Do you want to know if you should keep dating that guy you're talking to? Do you wish you could quit being afraid of what people will think about what you say or how you dress? Pray about your real struggles using Philippians 4:6-7 (NLT) and the prompts below.

"Do not be anxious about anything, but in every situation, by prayer and petition…"

When God says, "Do not be anxious about anything," He's inviting you to fear less and to experience His peace. Tell Him about a specific situation in your life that is stressful and exhausting. What are you most anxious about? Tell Him what that is.

Dear God, today I am anxious about _____

_____

"…with thanksgiving,"

Philippians 4 also tells us to thank the Lord when we pray about our fears (See the Fear LESS Fact on page 53 to help understand how this helps!) Tell the Lord what you are thankful for right now. It might be as simple as the sun shining or the food in your refrigerator. If you can't think of anything, take a minute to ask the Lord for help.

Father, thank you for _____

_____

"...present your requests to God."

What do you need from the Lord? What would help you fear less about this situation? Do you need confidence to tell your friend why you've been upset with her lately? Perhaps you want the Lord to help you decide what to study in school. Maybe you want to stop being afraid to leave your house. Tell the Lord your honest thoughts and ask Him for help (and keep asking!) You don't need to talk to Him a certain way; just "present your requests" and ask Him for peace regarding the test you'll take later today, that job you are considering, or anything else you need help with.

Jesus, here are my feelings and desires regarding this problem _____

_____

_____

_____

"Then you will experience God's peace, which exceeds anything we can understand. His peace will guard your hearts and minds as you live in Christ Jesus."

Faith is trusting God has done what His Word says He will, even when we can't see or feel it. Thank God for hearing your prayers and petitions, and ask Him to help you feel the peace He has for you.

Speaking of fill-in-the-blank, here's a blank page for you to write a prayer, draw a picture, or practice lettering a passage of Scripture. Enjoy!

F<small>EAR</small> LESS F<small>ACT</small>: "M<small>ULTIPLE STUDIES HAVE FOUND THAT PEOPLE WITH HIGHER LEVELS OF DISPOSITIONAL GRATITUDE</small> [<small>A NATURAL TENDENCY TO EXPRESS THANKFULNESS AND NOTICE THE POSITIVE</small>], <small>HAVE SIGNS OF BETTER PSYCHOLOGICAL HEALTH, INCLUDING HIGHER LEVELS OF PERCEIVED SOCIAL SUPPORT AND LOWER LEVELS OF STRESS, DEPRESSION, AND ANXIETY.</small>"[16] B<small>EFORE YOU FALL ASLEEP TONIGHT, THANK</small> G<small>OD FOR THREE THINGS.</small>

Day Eighteen

Me student teaching

WRESTLE

"I do believe; help me overcome my unbelief!"
Mark 9:24

If experiencing less fear happens the more you trust that God loves and delights in you, then part of "What now?" must include wrestling with the things you don't trust about Him. I am discipling a high school senior who told me that she believes God is real, but she told me she doesn't read the Bible because she finds it "boring and confusing." When I asked what she got out of praying, she said, "Absolutely nothing." I then asked what motivated her to believe in God when she didn't get anything from reading the Bible or praying. After thinking for a moment, she answered, "God wants me to talk to Him and build a relationship to help me somehow, but I haven't figured out how that happens or what it looks like."

I love young people. They aren't afraid to say what we're all thinking. They aren't the only ones who say they believe in God but don't read the Bible because it's confusing. They're not alone in wondering if prayer does anything or goes anywhere; they are just honest enough to admit it.

I know I keep saying it, but part of cooperating with the Spirit to fear less is continually increasing our trust in God. And it will be difficult to do that if we aren't reading the Bible (which is how He talks to us) or praying (which is how we talk to Him). Again, what kind of relationship would you have if you never talked or listened to your friend? And feeling guilty doesn't help or change things. A healthier way to thrive in a relationship, whether with humans or Jesus, is to be honest about why we struggle to communicate in the first place, and then prayerfully decide how to navigate what we discover.

As you wrestle with what you doubt or don't understand about God, be on the lookout for feelings of negativity or guilt. Remember, God is not condemning you (Romans 8:1). He loves and longs to welcome back those who have abandoned or disrespected Him (Luke 15:21-24). When we honestly and humbly seek answers about what we don't understand about God, He meets us where we are and addresses our questions with love and compassion (See Mark 9:17-27).

Something To Do

Think about your favorite worship song or Bible verse. Look up the lyrics to that song or passage of Scripture and ask yourself D.I.B.T. (Do I Believe That)? Do you believe the heartfelt and inspiring words on your beloved Elevation Worship playlist? Although Christian music is not the inerrant Word of God, we often feel closest to the Lord during worship. How often, however, do we think about whether or not we really believe what we're singing? When you post or pin a Bible verse, has it carried the same weight when times were tough? When my dad had a heart attack a few years back, I struggled to believe that God worked all things for the good of those who loved Him (Romans 8:28).

And remember, if you discover you don't believe those song lyrics or that Bible verse, persevere in asking the Lord to help you believe them more deeply. God cannot only handle our questions, according to the Bible, He welcomes them (Jeremiah 33:3, Matthew 7:7-8, Proverbs 2:3-5).

FEAR LESS FACT: AN OXFORD ACADEMIC ARTICLE REPORTED THAT "LISTENING TO RELIGIOUS MUSIC ALSO APPEARS TO MATTER FOR MENTAL HEALTH."[17] TODAY, ADD TO OR CREATE A WORSHIP PLAYLIST.

Day Nineteen

A father's love

READ CONTEXT

"There is no fear in love. But perfect love drives out fear, because fear has to do with punishment. The one who fears is not made perfect in love."
I John 4:18

When I first heard 1 John 4:18, I thought it meant that if I loved God more, I wouldn't struggle with anxiety. But since I was almost always afraid, this verse left me feeling guilty. I concluded that I must not love God enough. I felt condemned by it even though the Bible says Jesus doesn't condemn us (John 3:17). Sadly, even if we know and believe Jesus doesn't condemn us, most of us are experts at beating ourselves up. But there is hope; hope that we can receive God's grace, quit being unkind to ourselves, and fear less, too.

One of the most effective ways we will cooperate with the Holy Spirit in experiencing more peace is to avoid reading isolated Bible verses and instead read the whole passage. I'll admit I often struggle to discipline myself to read longer passages in the Bible. It takes time and mental energy. However, when we read one or two verses without reading the passages surrounding it, we risk reading the Bible in a way it wasn't intended and setting ourselves up for disappointment. More importantly, we risk reading the Bible in a way that causes us to misunderstand God's character and love.

If I had read all of 1 John 4, I would have realized that 1 John 4:10 says that what's more important than me loving God is knowing, "This is love: not that we loved God, but that he loved us." We can only love because God "first loved us" (vs. 19). The more I read, the more I realized I misunderstood 1 John 4:18a, "There is no fear in love." I thought that verse was about being fearless. I thought if I loved God more, I wouldn't have any fear. However, by reading the context and digging a bit into a commentary, I learned that 1 John 4:18a is talking about having no fear of judgment, not being *fearless*.[18]

1 John 4 isn't primarily about being fearless or loving God more. It is about knowing and receiving God's love for us. It is about continually reading the Bible and praying daily to know

and be reminded of God's perfect love in Jesus (vs. 9-10). Our job is simply to get to know His love more. The more we know and can accept Christ's heart for us, the more we will organically love and obey God and fear less. The more we read God's Word in context, the easier it will be to let Jesus remove a brick from our barriers of false protection. When that happens, we will experience more peace as we continually learn to trust His character.

Something To Do

Can you think of any Bible verses that you've read or heard that have made you feel guilty or like you don't have enough faith? A verse like Psalm 27:1, "The Lord is my light and my salvation—whom shall I fear? The Lord is the stronghold of my life—of whom shall I be afraid," has made me feel bad for struggling with anxiety. I've always read Matthew 14:31b when Jesus asks Peter after rescuing him from sinking, "'You of little faith,' he said, 'why did you doubt,'" like Jesus was disappointed with Peter.

Today, think of a verse about fear that's made you experience feelings of guilt or faithlessness. Then, read the whole chapter or story surrounding that verse. Look at Psalm 27:9 as David questions God's presence. Hear Matthew 14:31 as a loving invitation to the "more" Christ wanted for Peter. Write whatever passage you read in the fallen brick below; it is a fallen brick because any time we get a more accurate and comprehensive picture of God's love by reading His Word in context, the more His light and love will penetrate our barriers to peace.

Fear LESS Fact: New research from UC Berkeley confirms that "a sleepless night can trigger up to a 30% rise in anxiety levels."[19] Try going to bed half an hour earlier tonight than you usually do.

Day Twenty

Acting inappropriate in 1992

SEE YOUR HUMANNESS

"But the other criminal protested, 'Don't you fear God even when you have been sentenced to die? We deserve to die for our crimes, but this man hasn't done anything wrong.' Then he said, 'Jesus, remember me when you come into your Kingdom.' And Jesus replied, 'I assure you, today you will be with me in paradise.'"
Luke 23:40-42 (NLT)

One young woman I'm discipling just got friend-zoned by her boyfriend. She told me that she understands her identity and worth aren't contingent on that boy liking her, but she's still devastated. Although she knows that God says she's enough no matter who rejects her, she doesn't feel it in her heart. What she really wants is a hug and a dependable companion. Have you been there? I have.

What good does Jesus' love and acceptance "do" if I don't feel pretty or smart enough? How does God's grace help me if I'm afraid something's wrong with me because I don't have a boyfriend or worry that I'll hate my job? How can I trust or care what God says about me if I struggle to like myself?

The common threads in this list are the words "me" and "I." Underneath our problems are the deeply seated fears that we're broken and not enough. And although we're all made in God's image, the struggles of life remind us that sin has fractured humankind. But even if we believe Christ has redeemed our brokenness, we may still wonder how the cross helps us when we feel rejected and alone. So, *What now?*

Something to Do

As counterintuitive as it sounds, acknowledging our hopelessness apart from the cross can help us navigate the rejection of others, and fear less. However, saying, "I'm a mess," isn't concrete or beneficial. We want to identify where specifically we feel broken and hopeless. (And yes, this is as terrible an exercise as it sounds, but getting concrete is worth the freedom it can bring.)

Underneath the cross below, write down mistakes you've made and what you don't like about yourself. Jot down failures and embarrassing things you've done on the fallen bricks. A few of mine include my SAT score, bad memory, and the inappropriate relationships I had in college. As you add bricks to the foot of the cross, think about Jesus. What does He look like as you lay your sins and shame at His feet? Is He compassionate? Sad? Loving? Angry? Disappointed? We'll talk more about that tomorrow, but for now, take your time and don't rush through this powerful exercise.

FEAR LESS FACT: "ADEQUATE AMOUNTS OF SOCIAL SUPPORT ARE ASSOCIATED WITH INCREASES IN LEVELS OF A HORMONE CALLED OXYTOCIN, WHICH FUNCTIONS TO DECREASE ANXIETY LEVELS."[20] TODAY, SPEND TIME WITH YOUR FAMILY OR A FRIEND OR GO TO CHURCH.

Day Twenty-one

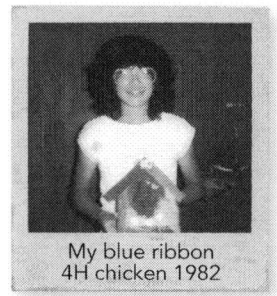

My blue ribbon
4H chicken 1982

KNOW THE REAL JESUS

"For God did not send his Son into the world to condemn the world, but to save the world through him."
John 3:17

How did your time at the cross go yesterday? Was it guilt-inducing? Embarrassing? Freeing? I experienced so many thoughts and emotions when I did this exercise. At the time, I'd been learning more about Jesus by reading the Bible. Before that, Jesus was who I'd made Him up to be or who people told me He was. I thought that my behavior was His primary concern. (It is not.) Reading about the real Jesus in the Bible, who loved and forgave me, was revolutionary. But unfortunately, receiving that forgiveness was difficult.

Why? Because most of us, even if we think of Jesus as loving and forgiving, don't believe it deep within our hearts. How do I know that? Well, it goes back to how we talk to and about ourselves. Jesus died so that no one, not even you, can call you lazy, ugly, or stupid. If we believed that deeply, we wouldn't talk about ourselves, jokingly or seriously, in ways Jesus never would.

However, exercises like the one in the last chapter can help us pay attention to the disconnect between what we deeply believe and what we only partly believe about Jesus. They can also help make vague beliefs more concrete and guide us toward knowing the real, biblical Jesus in new ways that will help us fear less. How? The good news is, you are doing the how. More about that in the next chapter. For now, more about the real Jesus.

Something to Do

In the last chapter, you wrote down some bad choices you've made, and things you don't like about yourself. This time, write down all the good things you've done. What do you like about yourself? What are you good at? Write them on the bricks like you did yesterday, but this time, picture Jesus on the cross as you bring your awards and talents to His feet. What is His expression? Does He say anything to you?

Take your time with this activity, even if it is difficult or embarrassing. The good things about you are wonderful gifts to be celebrated. However, as we talked about earlier, the things we do, whether good or bad, don't define us. We are loved, chosen, and delighted in because Jesus loves and died for us, not because we fail or succeed. Only the real Jesus can love you like that.

Fear LESS Fact: The FDA reports that fifty percent of people don't take the medications prescribed to them.[21] If your doctor has prescribed medication for your anxiety, thyroid, or ADHD, be sure you take it as directed.

Day Twenty-Two

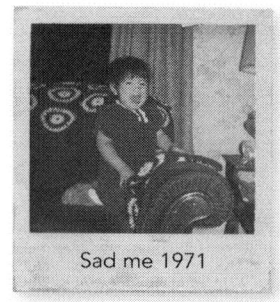
Sad me 1971

REMEMBER A RESCUE

*"He lifted me out of the slimy pit, out of the mud and mire;
he set my feet on a rock and gave me a firm place to stand."*
Psalm 40:2

How are you doing? Are you wondering how anything you've done so far relates to your anxiety problems? Although I will try and continue to articulate how knowing God's love and grace translates into learning how to fear less, the bad news is, I can't totally do that without help from the Spirit.

So much of how I learned to open myself up to the Lord in learning to fear less is difficult to put into words. My experience is not like a math equation that you can reproduce to get the same results. The Holy Spirit must do His good, slow work so we can fear less. But what do we do when we're struggling with fear and don't feel like the Spirit is helping? What do we do while we wait and wonder?

I remember a time years ago when I was in the throes of a panic attack. I kept praying and asking God for help. But He didn't. I begged and begged, but nothing happened. That wasn't the first time that's happened to me, and unfortunately, it probably won't be the last.

Although the Lord lovingly removes one brick at a time from our wall of fear and false protection, whether we feel it or not, waiting for and recognizing His grace in that process isn't easy. Sometimes, I've prayed and prayed and waited and prayed some more and felt "absolutely nothing," as my friend put it. And that's frustrating and difficult. Sometimes, we need to just acknowledge that without fixing or over-spiritualizing it. Eventually, however, it's good to ask again, *What now?*

Something to Do

Read Psalm 142. Then, as David did, write about a difficult time you went through and how God was faithful in that season. In other words, remember a time when the Lord rescued you.

Maybe it was when you first believed in Jesus or a time you felt His presence when you were otherwise alone and broken.

Most of the laments in the Bible, like Psalm 142, end with a reminder of God's faithfulness. They are raw and painful but return to a time when the Lord rescued His children. The Exodus narrative, where God rescued the Israelites from slavery and parted the Red Sea, "is the most frequently mentioned event in the entire Old Testament, referred to over 120 times."[22] Recalling a time the Lord has rescued us will remind us of His goodness and unchanging love when we can't see it and are questioning if we believe it.

If you're unsure about what you believe about God or haven't felt God's rescue, I encourage you to read Psalm 142 a few times and see if it makes you feel a little better, even if you aren't sure what you believe.

Fear LESS Fact: An American Heart Association "study of more than 2,500 people ages 13-24 found that nicotine-only vapers, THC-only vapers and dual vapers (of nicotine and THC) were more likely to report anxiety symptoms, depressive symptoms and suicidal thoughts when compared with their peers who did not use electronic cigarettes or vape THC."[23] If you vape and want to quit, check out teen.smokefree.gov.

Day Twenty-three

Barb and me
22 years ago

FIND A FRIEND

*"Aaron and Hur held his hands up—one on one side, one on the other—
so that his hands remained steady till sunset."*
Exodus 17:12b

One of the more practical ways we can fear less is to be intentional about spending time with friends who can lovingly speak peace into our lives. My friend Barb is one of those friends for me. Although she wrestles with anxiety, too, Barb is someone I can "receive" peace from.

What do I mean by that? Well, sometimes people with good intentions offer me advice about how to deal with my anxiety, but because Barb has struggled with fear and anxiety, I know she understands. She is someone I can hear without getting defensive or being dismissive toward. When she kindly assures me that my back pain isn't a sure sign that my kidneys are failing, I know she's not being flippant or condescending. Because Barb and I have been friends and prayer partners for years, when she tells me that the noise in my car doesn't mean that my wheel is going to fall off, her counsel is a gift to me and has often helped me to fear less.

It is also helpful to be purposeful about spending time with friends who do not gravitate to fear as easily, quickly, or often as we do. My husband is that friend for me. I have often told him I wished I could live in his head for five minutes because it seems like the most relaxing and stress-free place on earth. In reality, my husband has fears and anxieties, but they aren't about the things I'm worried about and don't manifest themselves in the same way or frequency.

Friends who fear less help me ask myself Philippians 4:8 more often; is what I'm worrying about true? Is it true my blood test results mean I have an incurable disease or an unanswered text guarantees something bad has happened? And pondering truth helps me make room for the rest of the wisdom found in Philippians 4:8, thinking about things that are "excellent and praiseworthy." Dwelling on good and Godly realities instead of hypothetical untruths, can help us fear less, too.

Something to Do

Who are a few friends you trust? Who is someone who doesn't try to fix your fears, but points you back to Jesus' love and reminds you that He can and desires to help you with your anxieties? Who are a few people you love who aren't as quick to feel anxious as you are? Write their names on the fallen brick below. These friends and family members are gifts to help you feel God's light and love more by helping you fear less. You might also want to write down or think of ways to spend more time with these friends in the coming year. Perhaps you could do a Bible study or read a book together. Maybe you can work out together or grab coffee once every three months.

If you do not have a friend or a few friends like this, spend some time asking the Lord for a friend who fears less! The Lord was the first one to acknowledge that it was not good for us to be alone (Genesis 2:18), so trust that He desires this kind of friend for you even more than you do.

FEAR LESS FACT: AN "ENDOCRINE SOCIETY STUDY SAYS THAT A 30-MINUTE POWER NAP CAN HELP TO REVERSE THE EFFECTS OF A POOR NIGHT'S SLEEP."[24] WE ALREADY READ ABOUT THE WAYS SLEEP HELPS ANXIETY, SO GO TAKE A POWER NAP. (MY WISE JAPANESE MOTHER SAYS EVEN IF YOU JUST LAY DOWN AND CLOSE YOUR EYES WITHOUT FALLING ASLEEP, YOU'LL FEEL BETTER AFTERWARD.) TRY TO SQUEEZE A POWER NAP IN SOMETIME TODAY!

Day Twenty-four

12,500 feet up in CO

WATCH THE NEWS

"Fix your thoughts on what is true, and honorable, and right, and pure, and lovely, and admirable. Think about things that are excellent and worthy of praise."
Philippians 4:8b (NLT)

I struggle with the news. It is depressing and violent, and I often feel worse after watching it. When I was young, the news often triggered panic attacks. My skin still crawls a little if I hear the intro music on TV. However, one of the ways the Lord's helped me fear less has been to watch the news occasionally.

When I watch the news, I'm prompted to pray for people who, unlike me, live in unimaginable poverty or where natural disasters abound. As I pray, I also shift my focus off from myself, which helps me to fear less, too. Although I know my life isn't as difficult as many people's, I often forget that. Periodically reading the news helps me pray for others and makes my "first-world problems" more concrete.

Once, my husband and I were taking a company trip to Colorado. Instead of being excited, I was filled with fear. Since we were traveling without our kids, I worried about who'd parent them if our plane crashed. We were also going to go skiing, but I'm deathly afraid of heights. I knew we'd also be traveling on icy mountain passes. Although I'm not afraid of where I'll go after I die, careening down a hill to get there sounds unpleasant. I wanted to be thankful, but as fear always does, it robbed me of enjoying life.

However, I'd recently read about a boy who was battling cancer. His family had flown around the country for his treatments. En route to the airport, the Spirit brought the boy to mind. After praying and weeping for him and his family, I realized I could be traveling not for fun, but for chemotherapy. Instead of having a relaxing vacation, I could be trying to save my son.

When I pray for people I've seen on the news who have such unthinkable situations, it shifts my focus from my own worries onto the Lord and the people who desperately need His hope and healing. It helps me think once again about what is true, excellent, and praiseworthy, as Philippians 4 admonishes, instead of what Bible teacher Beth Moore calls the "what I.F.'s" (what I Fear).

Knowing that other people are suffering or have worse problems than us isn't an exercise in shame or self-deprecation. Nor should those things diminish or induce guilt surrounding our own struggles and anxieties. However, like King David in 2 Samuel 19, we can become so consumed by our own pain that we can miss caring for those around us. And in His loving generosity, God often blesses us with His peace as we empathize with and love others.

Something to Do

Find a story about someone who's struggling. Maybe the person is sick or homeless. Write a prayer below for that person. Ask God to remind them of His love and peace, even if they can't see or feel either in the storm they're facing.

Then, write three things you're grateful for on the fallen bricks below. Remember that gratitude helps lessen our anxiety, which also creates mental and emotional space to pray for those around us. And don't forget that prayer and thankfulness allow God's light to penetrate the wall we're still hiding behind—a wall that's getting smaller and less important to us the more we trust the Lord and His love.

FEAR LESS FACT: ONE OF THE HARDEST ASSIGNMENTS I GIVE WOMEN ON THEIR JOURNEY TO FEAR LESS IS TO "BE STILL AND KNOW" THAT GOD IS GOD (PSALM 46:10). TODAY, USE THE ONE MINUTE PAUSE APP (PAUSEAPP.COM) TO ENJOY DOING NOTHING FOR ONE MINUTE.

Day Twenty-five

Me being BRAVE on my bike

MAKE A LIST

*"For God has not given us a spirit of fear,
but of power and of love and of a sound mind."*
2 Timothy 1:7 (NKJV)

Because I've battled anxiety for so long, I used to talk and joke a lot about my fears. I would warn people I was traveling with or meeting for the first time that I wasn't a risk taker. I would share about my fear of caves and tidal waves. I tried to ensure that people didn't expect me to do anything scary. For many years, I have talked about my fears, but talking about them is different than wondering, *What now?* Asking, *What now?* has taught me two things that have helped me to fear less.

The first lesson I've learned is that it's not true that I'm always afraid. Yes, I've battled panic attacks, and the thought of being in a submarine makes me start to sweat. But it isn't true that I'm afraid of everything or all the time. And it's not true about you either.

Interestingly, I've noticed that the more I talk about my anxieties, the more fearful and paranoid I seem to be. Of course, I process fears and secrets buried in my boxes with close friends. However, I'm learning one way to fear less is not to give constant attention to my anxieties or let them define me.

The second thing I've been realizing is that some of the things I'm not afraid of, other people are. This might sound silly or obvious, but for those of us who feel like wimps, I think that a helpful way to start to fear less is to recognize where you already do. For example, I love biking. Even after I fell off my bike and broke my knee and wrist a year and a half ago, with the Lord's help, I still love cycling, and I'm not (very) afraid of falling. However, a friend told me she's always been afraid to ride a bike. The thought had never occurred to me that someone would be afraid of something I loved so much. Realizing that has been empowering and emboldening.

Something to Do

Whether you feel or believe it, the Bible says God hasn't given you a spirit of fear but a spirit of power, love, and sound mind (2 Timothy 1:7). List the things you aren't afraid to do on the fallen bricks below. Also, include the things you used to be afraid of that don't bother you anymore.

Then, write on the lines below something you do that requires strength (mental, emotional, or physical strength). Write down something you've done that was loving and situations where you've needed to use your smart and sound mind to take a test or fix your computer. Start stepping into the spirit of power, love, and sound mind the Lord has given you by making a list. As you write, remember you are cooperating with the Spirit in loosening bricks, slowly but surely.

FEAR LESS FACT: "STUDIES HAVE FOUND THAT COLLEGE STUDENTS WHO ARE DEPENDENT ON THEIR CELL PHONES ARE MORE LIKELY TO EXPERIENCE ANXIETY DURING TIME AWAY FROM THEIR PHONE, AS WELL AS DURING LEISURE TIME. INDIVIDUALS OFTEN REPORT HIGHER LEVELS OF DEPRESSION AND ANXIETY RELATED TO SOCIAL MEDIA USAGE DUE TO FEELING LEFT OUT, COMPARING THEMSELVES TO OTHERS, ETC."[25] TONIGHT, PUT YOUR PHONE IN ANOTHER ROOM BEFORE YOU FALL ASLEEP.

Day Twenty-six

Glasses!

GET NEW GLASSES

*"This means that anyone who belongs to Christ has become a new person.
The old life is gone; a new life has begun!"*
2 Corinthians 5:17 (NLT)

Throughout this devotional, I've tried to emphasize that I had panic attacks for many years before the Lord freed me from them and that I still battle fear. Yet some people think that because I'm a Bible teacher, the process was easier for me than it might be for someone who isn't in ministry or didn't go to seminary. However, I didn't remotely begin to understand what it meant to be a Christian until I was in my late twenties.

Prior to having a relationship with Jesus Christ, although I'd always gone to church, I mistakenly thought being a Christian was about avoiding bad things and doing good things more often. I also thought that being a Christian meant that praying and going to church would result in my life being easier, and when it wasn't, I was confused. I was also baffled about the Bible because, growing up, God's Word was one of two extremes—either a book only a pastor could touch or a judgmental list of rules to follow perfectly. Being a Christian wasn't about believing in Jesus' death and resurrection, but a lot of do's and do not's.

So not only did my brick wall include a lot of fears and ways I coped with them, but it also had many bricks about God and the Bible that were inaccurate and biblically unbalanced. And since God didn't seem to "work" in getting rid of my anxiety, I resorted to many other ways to find my worth and try to fear less. Things that are embarrassing to admit even thirty years later.

However, remember that part of how we let God dismantle our brick walls is by seeing our humanness and mistakes and remembering that Jesus died because we will fail. One of the best ways to live out *What now?* and dismantle some of our barriers to peace is to continually change the lens through which we view ourselves. In order to fear less, we must repeatedly re-examine our focus. Are we reverting to seeing ourselves based on what someone said about us growing up, or do we see ourselves as Jesus does? Is our focus on who Jesus says we are because He died for us, or is it rooted in our ability to prove those things consistently and perfectly (when that's impossible according to Romans 3:23)? We must put on gospel-centered glasses every morning to preach the cross to ourselves daily.

Something to Do

On the glasses below, write in pencil everything you regret and wish you could change about yourself. I regret the relationships and partying I did in college. I hate my big feet and social anxiety. I have a terrible memory, and I'm jealous of people who I think are prettier and more successful than I am. I could easily fill up these glasses.

Now, I want you to Google "who God says I am." Use a marker to write all the words the Bible uses to describe you over the penciled words you filled in about yourself. Ask God to help you believe that He sees you through these lenses even when you're at your worst—whether you gossiped yesterday about your pastor's wife or partied last weekend like it was 1999.

Why do we need His help with this? Because although Jesus Christ's death on the cross redeemed us from our sins and failures, we instinctively revert to forgetting that truth. We are righteous because we believe in Him, not because we're awesome. (See Romans 4:5 if you don't believe me.) But we need His help believing that daily. As you write the truth of who you are below, listen for the sound of bricks falling.

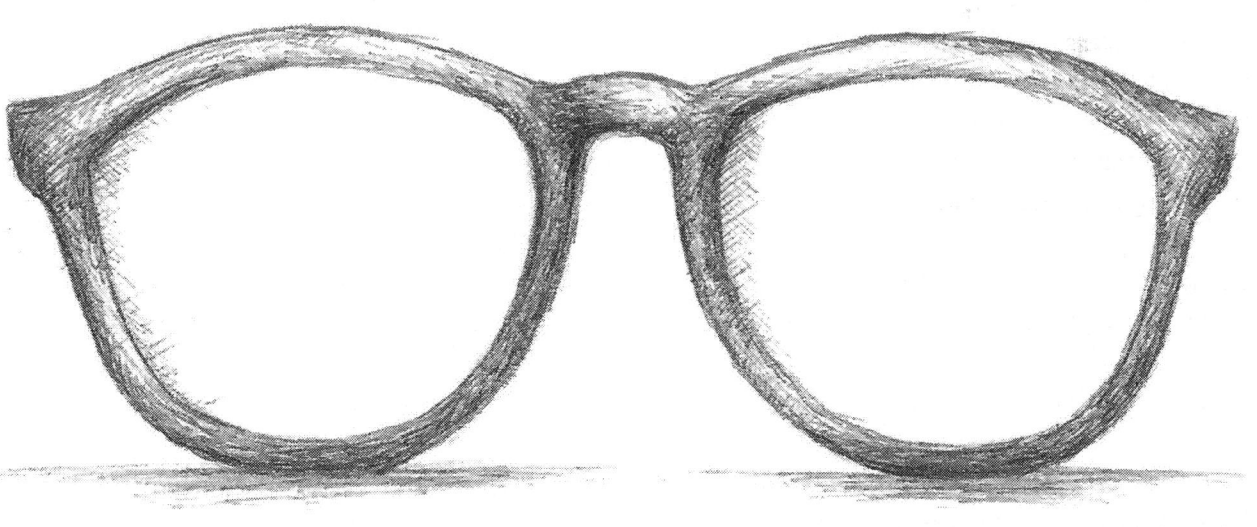

FEAR LESS FACT: "STUDIES SHOW THAT PEOPLE WHO ENGAGE IN SELF-CARE REPORT LOWER LEVELS OF STRESS AND IMPROVED QUALITY OF LIFE, WHILE A LACK OF SELF-CARE IS ASSOCIATED WITH HIGHER RISK OF STRESS AND BURNOUT."[26] DO SOMETHING JUST FOR YOU TODAY LIKE TAKE A BATH, LIGHT A CANDLE, OR GO FOR A WALK.

Day Twenty-seven

Driving to the Northwoods

TRUST REDEMPTION

"Praise be to the God and Father of our Lord Jesus Christ, the Father of compassion and the God of all comfort, who comforts us in all our troubles, so that we can comfort those in any trouble with the comfort we ourselves receive from God."
2 Corinthians 1:3-4

When my kids were growing up, perhaps my most frequent prayer was for the Lord to spare them from battling the anxiety and panic attacks I had. However, as I mentioned earlier, at different points in my children's lives, they have struggled with fear and anxiety. However, not only have I come to the place where I can honestly say I trust God's love and goodness despite that, I recently realized how their struggles might even be a blessing in disguise.

Shortly after one of my kids told me they had been struggling with panic attacks, I was headed to teach at a Bible camp in northern Wisconsin. During my five-hour drive, I had a considerable amount of time to worry and pray about my adult child, who wasn't sure how to traverse their debilitating anxiety. I felt terrible and wanted to take their fear away somehow. Obviously, I knew I had no power to do that. So, I continued to pray and renew my mind by reciting Scripture that reminded me God was good and in control.

After the retreat, I was driving home and thinking about how much I love sharing Jesus with women. I felt overjoyed, realizing what a gift it is to do what I do. As I drove, I realized that if it hadn't been for my struggles with fear and anxiety, I never would have left my teaching career and started in ministry. I wouldn't have started speaking about how the Lord had helped me with my panic attacks. And I wouldn't have the faith in Christ that I have today had it not been for the terrible thing I was praying the Lord would remove immediately from my child's life, fear.

I hate anxiety and do not wish it on anyone, but thankfully, Christ came to redeem what is broken in this world, which means nothing, not even our fears, are ever wasted. Being reminded that it was anxiety that changed the trajectory of my own career and faith gave me perspective about my kids' fears and struggles.

Dear one, I hope the reminder that your struggles with anxiety will not be wasted causes you to hear another brick falling out of your now very holey wall. God has greater peace and purpose for you as you trust Him more and, brick by brick, fear less.

Something to Do

How have your fears and struggles with anxiety helped your faith in Jesus Christ grow? Can you recall a time when you were afraid but experienced more peace after reading the Bible or praying? Has your journey with anxiety led you to encourage or pray for another person struggling with fear? Write about that experience below and thank the Lord for ensuring that nothing is ever wasted in our lives for those who believe in Him.

If you haven't ever experienced God's peace or felt closer to Christ, I encourage you to tell the Lord that. Although the Lord's peace isn't always felt instantly, He meets us in our questions and doubts when we patiently and persistently seek and trust Him more.

Fear LESS Fact: "A lack of vitamin D may also play a role in the development of various mental health disorders," including depression and anxiety.[27] Ask a parent or your doctor if you're getting enough vitamin D.

Day Twenty-eight

Teaching women to Fear LESS

REPEAT

*"You will keep in perfect peace all who trust in you,
all whose thoughts are fixed on you!"*
Isaiah 26:3 (NLT)

Although we will never be completely fearless, we can discover and dismantle some of the barriers that fear has surrounded us with, in order to fear less. Knowing where we don't trust God and His love helps us evaluate the why behind our fears. Reading God's Word, praying, and wrestling through our doubts and questions about Him also helps us to fear less. Being kinder to ourselves and talking to and about ourselves as Jesus would, helps us know the real Jesus and experience His grace in our struggles and anxieties.

The ways to fear less are endless. According to Ephesians 3:18, we cannot exhaust knowing the width, length, height, and depth of Christ's love for us. Paul reminds us that we can be filled to overflowing by God's love. There is always more room to fear less because there is always more of God's love to know and experience. It took me almost thirty years before the Lord freed me from panic attacks. Although you fear less today than you did twenty-eight days ago, God has more freedom for you!

After completing my phone devotional last month, I checked my average phone usage. It wasn't at zero minutes. It's not even at an hour a day. But it's down from the four hours I was on it before I started the devotional to around two hours of usage a day. I have not thrown my phone away, but I'm using it less. 2 Peter 1:5-7 reminds us that we can possess more things like goodness, perseverance, and love in *increasing measure*. Not perfectly or all at one time, but slowly and gradually, one brick at a time.

Something To Do
Think about all the Bible verses about fear and anxiety you've read in the past twenty-eight days. Which passage felt the most inviting? Which one do you find yourself trying to remember?

Look back and find that verse. Write it in the space below and on several Post-it notes. Ask the Lord to help you memorize it.

If I had to identify the single most helpful way I opened myself up to receive more peace from the Lord over the past fifty years, I would say it was memorizing verses like Philippians 4:6-8 and 2 Timothy 1:7. If you commit even one verse to memory from God's Word, it will become such a precious gift to you in learning to fear less that you will want to learn others.

It is not magic or instant. Sometimes, you will doubt if knowing it matters or makes a difference. Sometimes, you will say it during a panic attack, and it won't change anything as far as you can tell. But if you repeat God's Word when you least feel like it or don't know if it "works," I promise you that simple practice will help you trust God's love and delight in you, and in that, you will not be able to help but fear less.

Fear LESS Fact: The Bible says "'Though the mountains be shaken and the hills be removed, yet my unfailing love for you will not be shaken nor my covenant of peace be removed,' says the Lord, who has compassion on you (Isaiah 54:10)." Look back at Day Two. What was your response to the question about the one fear you'd most like to fear less right now? Thank God that His covenant of peace and compassion are helping you fear less and will continue to do so as you cling to His unfailing love for you.

BIBLIOGRAPHY

1   Loeuy, K. J. (2022, April 11). The Whole U University of Washington. Retrieved from https://thewholeu.uw.edu/2022/01/11/art-for-self-care-and-mental-health.

2   Princing, M. (2021, September 1). Right as Rain by WU Medicine. Retrieved from https://rightasrain.uwmedicine.org/mind/stress/why-deep-breathing-makes-you-feel-so-chill.

3   Uma Naidoo, M. (2020, October 27). health.harvard.edu. Retrieved from Harvard Health Publishing: https://www.health.harvard.edu/blog/eating-well-to-help-manage-anxiety-your-questions-answered-2018031413460#:~:text=Avoiding%20processed%20foods%20and%20foods,can%20mimic%20a%20panic%20attack.

4   Novotney, A. (2019, May). apa.org. Retrieved from American Pyschological Association: https://www.apa.org/monitor/2019/05/ce-corner-isolation.

5   Zhao, J., Yin, H., Zhang, G., Li, G., Shang, B., Wang, C., & Chen, L. (2019, May 9). National Library of Medicine. Retrieved from https://pubmed.ncbi.nlm.nih.gov/30882915/.

6   Gillihan, S. J. (2017, October 10). Psychology Today. Retrieved from https://www.psychologytoday.com/us/blog/think-act-be/201710/how-helping-others-can-relieve-anxiety-and-depression.

7   Cuncic, A. M. (2021, October21). Verywell Mind. Retrieved from https://www.verywellmind.com/talk-people-social-anxiety-disorder-3024390.

8   Aquin, J. P., El-Gabalawy, R., Sala, T., & Sareen, J. M. (2017, April 6). National Library of Medicine. Retrieved from https://www.ncbi.nlm.nih.gov/pmc/articles/PMC6526963/.

9   Ortlund, D. (2020). *Gentle and Lowly.* Wheaton: Crossway. pg. 151.

10   Adams-Colon, B. (2021, June 23). Colorado State University. Retrieved from Columbine Health Systems Center for Healthy Aging: https://www.research.colostate.edu/healthyagingcenter/2021/06/23/the-simple-act-of-stretching/#:~:text=Stretching%20reduces%20the%20muscle%20tension,decrease%20in%20depression%20and%20anxiety.

11   Redding, S. (2020, May 5). Michigan Medicine University of Michigan. Retrieved from https://www.michiganmedicine.org/health-lab/using-music-times-anxiety.

12   Haghighatdoost, F., Feizi, A., Esmaillzadeh, A., Rashidi-Pourfard, N., Keshteli, A. H., Roohafza, H., & Adibi, P. (2018, September 20). National Library of Medicine. Retrieved from https://www.ncbi.nlm.nih.gov/pmc/articles/PMC6147771/.

13   Shafer, L. (2017, December 15). Harvard Graduate School of Education. Retrieved from gse.harvard.edu: https://www.gse.harvard.edu/news/uk/17/12/social-media-and-teen-anxiety.

14   Ratey, J. J. (2019, October 24). Harvard Health Publishing. Retrieved from health.harvard.edu: https://www.health.harvard.edu/blog/can-exercise-help-treat-anxiety-2019102418096.

15   Beutell, C. A. (2022, December). Northwestern Medicine. Retrieved from https://www.nm.org/healthbeat/healthy-tips/health-benefits-of-having-a-routine#:~:text=An%20effective%20routine%20can%20help,emotional%20well%2Dbeing%20and%20energy.

16   Allen, S. P. (2018, May). Greater Good Science Center. Retrieved from ggsc.berkeley.edu: https://ggsc.berkeley.edu/images/uploads/GGSC-JTF_White_Paper-Gratitude-FINAL.pdf.

17   Bradshaw, M. P., Ellison, C. G., & Fang, Q. M. (2014, April 15). The Gerontologist. Retrieved from Oxford Academic: https://academic.oup.com/gerontologist/article/55/6/961/2605451.

18   Keener, C. S. (2014). *The IVP Bible Background Commentary.* Downer's Grove: InterVarsity Press. pg. 714.

19   Anwar, Y. (2019, November 4). Berkely News. Retrieved from https://news.berkeley.edu/2019/11/04/deep-sleep-can-rewire-the-anxious-brain/.

20   Mental Help Net. (n.d.). Retrieved from https://www.mentalhelp.net/stress/socialization-and-altruistic-acts-as-stress-relief/#:~:text=Adequate%20amounts%20of%20social%20support,nervous%20system%20calming%20down%20responses.

21   US Food and Drug Administration. (2016, February 16). Retrieved from https://www.fda.gov/drugs/special-features/why-you-need-take-your-medications-prescribed-or-instructed#:~:text=Medication%20is%20not%20taken%20as%20prescribed%2050%20percent%20of%20the%20time.

22   Windle, B. (2021, September 24). Bible Archaeology Report. Retrieved from https://biblearchaeologyreport.com/2021/09/24/top-ten-discoveries-related-to-moses-and-the-exodus/.

23   Newsroom. (2023, February 28). Retrieved from https://newsroom.heart.org/news/depression-anxiety-symptoms-linked-to-vaping-nicotine-and-thc-in-teens-and-young-adults.

24   Schuldt, B. (2016, February 10). LSA Psychology University of Michigan. Retrieved from https://lsa.umich.edu/psych/news-events/all-news/graduate-news/what-happened-when-i-took-a-power-nap-every-day-for-a-week-.html#:~:text=Studies%20show%20that%20taking%20a,is%20easier%20said%20than%20done.

25   Gardner, E. L. (2022, June 2). Online-Therapy.com. Retrieved from https://www.online-therapy.com/blog/is-your-phone-causing-anxiety/#easy-footnote-5-13207.

26   Kubala, J. R.-B., & Jennings, K.-A. M. (2023, July 12). Healthline. Retrieved from https://www.healthline.com/nutrition/16-ways-relieve-stress-anxiety#5.-Practice-self-care.

27   Pedersen, T. (2022, April 8). PsychCentral. Retrieved from https://psychcentral.com/blog/does-vitamin-d-deficiency-impact-mental-health.

RESOURCES

The following list is a small sampling of resources available to help with anxiety and anxiety-related issues. They are not intended to replace medical, clinical, or professional advice, diagnosis, or medical intervention.

Suicide Prevention and Crisis Counseling

National Suicide Prevention Lifeline: 1-800-273-8255 Provides 24/7 free and confidential support for people in distress, prevention and crisis resources, and best practices for professionals.

SUICIDE HELP: 988 Suicide and Crisis Lifeline, 988lifeline.org, or dial 9-1-1.

Text HOME to 741741 to connect with a volunteer Crisis Counselor 24/7 at the Crisis Text Line. crisistextline.org

Christian Crisis, Mental Health, and Sexuality Resources

Living Hope Ministries
Provides a safe place for individuals wrestling questions of faith and sexuality through weekly support groups, moderated online forms, in-depth discipleship programs, and active partnerships with churches around the world.
PO Box 2239 Arlington, TX 76004
817-459-2507
livehope.org

Lighthouse Network
The #1 Christian Mental Health and Sex Addiction Helpline in the United States.
lighthousenetwork.org
844-543-3242

Vaping and Substance Abuse Resources

teen.smokefree.gov

Substance Abuse and Mental Health Services

Free National Helpline 1-800-662-HELP (4357)
samhsa.gov

ABOUT THE AUTHOR

Laura Sandretti is a Bible teacher, women's conference and retreat speaker, and author. She has a Master of Arts in Theological Studies and is a former high school teacher and women's ministry director. Laura leads discipleship groups and a moms group at a crisis pregnancy center in Milwaukee, WI. She also writes for *Just Between Us*, an international ministry magazine for women. In her free time, she loves biking, hiking, and hanging out with her husband and four adult children, and her perfect dog, Dexter. *Four Weeks to Fear LESS* is Laura's fourth book.

You can find out more about Laura at laurasandretti.com.

Made in the USA
Monee, IL
02 March 2024

54033972R00049